EC Media Law

CW01391379

■ EUROPEAN LAW SERIES ■

Series Editor:
PROFESSOR JOHN A. USHER

Published Titles

International Relations Law of the European Union
DOMINIC McGOLDRICK

EC Public Procurement Law
CHRISTOPHER BOVIS

EC Insurance Law
ROBERT MERKIN AND ANGUS RODGER

EC Consumer Law and Policy
STEPHEN WEATHERILL

EC Tax Law
DAVID WILLIAMS

General Principles of EC Law
JOHN A. USHER

EU Law and Human Rights
LAMMY BETTEN and NICHOLAS GRIEF

EC Environmental Law
JOANNE SCOTT

EC Institutions and Legislation
JOHN A. USHER

European Social Law and Policy
TAMARA HERVEY

EC Media Law and Policy
DAVID GOLDBERG, TONY PROSSER, STEFAAN VERHULST

Civil Jurisdiction and Judgments
PETER STONE

EC Media Law and Policy

DAVID GOLDBERG, TONY PROSSER,
STEFAAN VERHULST

LONGMAN
LONDON AND NEW YORK

Addison Wesley Longman Limited,
Edinburgh Gate,
Harlow,
Essex CM20 2JE,
United Kingdom
and Associated Companies throughout the world.

First published 1998

ISBN 0-582-31266-3 PPR

Visit Addison Wesley Longman on the world wide web at
<http://www.awl-he.com>

British Library Cataloguing-in-Publication Data

A catalogue record for this book is available from the British Library

Set in Sabon
Printed in Malaysia, LSP

Contents

Preface   vii

General Editor's Preface   ix

Table of Cases   xi

Table of Directives   xiii

Table of Web Sites   xv

Table of Abbreviations   xvii

Table of Equivalence after Treaty of Amsterdam   xix

1   Introduction   1

2   Foundations of Community Media Policy   8
    Introduction and policy rationales   8
    The competence issue   11
    Foundation texts   15
    The European institutions, their interests and their
        impact   20

3   The Pan-European Context   25
    The Council of Europe   25
    The Organization for Security and Cooperation in
        Europe   38
    European Broadcasting Union   39
    European Platform of Regulatory Authorities (EPRA)   40
    The European Radiocommunications Office   40
    Conclusion   41

4   Origins of European Community Media Policy   42
    1980–84: The Parliament's concerns   42
    The Green Paper   45
    Support systems for the audiovisual industry   51
    Conclusion   54

5   The *Television Without Frontiers* Directive   56

6   Other Legal Measures and Support Mechanisms   76
    Satellite and Cable   76
    Content regulation in newer audiovisual services 79
    Support actions for the programme industry   79
    The MAC legacy and standardisation   83
    Copyright   86
    Competition policy and media ownership   88
    Commercial communications   93
    Conclusion   95

7   The information society   96
    The Bangemann Report and Action Plan   97
    New priorities   99
    International conferences   101
    Regulatory transparency   103
    The information society and telecommunications
        policy   104
    Funding programmes   109
    Social aspects of the information society   111
    The Convergence Green Paper   114
    The media and data protection   117
    Conclusion   120

8   Conclusions   122

Further reading   129
Bibliography   130
Index   135

Preface

This book aims to provide a reasonably comprehensive account of the law and policy of the European Community in the media or audiovisual fields. These are widely defined to include the so-called 'new' media and the developments towards an 'information society' through the convergence of broadcasting, telecommunications and computing. It also describes briefly the various support measures developed for the media industries in order to provide a complete picture and to provide a context for the regulatory actions described.

It will rapidly become apparent that European media law and policy are not noted for their coherence. Not only is there a range of different types of medium, but the rationales and legal foundations of Community action are various and contested. There is also institutional conflict within the Community Institutions and between Member States which complicate the picture further. Nevertheless, we shall suggest that, with some exceptions, the regulatory approach taken has been largely successful and has anticipated future developments in this ever-changing world more clearly than have many national governments.

The book draws upon work funded by the Economic and Social Research Council (grant no. L126251021) as part of its Media Economics and Media Culture Research Programme; the bulk of that work is published separately but the grant did permit us to develop our study of Community policies.[1] We would like to thank the Council for its support, especially the Director of the

---

1. Goldberg, D., Prosser, T. and Verhulst, S., *Regulating the Changing Media: A Comparative Study*, Clarendon, 1998.

Programme, Professor Simon Frith. We would also like to thank the Faculty of Law and Financial Studies at the University of Glasgow for some financial support to enable a brief continuation of work after the Research Council fund had ended. The project administrator was Gill Kane and her contribution was essential in achieving the goals of the research. We would also like to thank the European Audiovisual Observatory in Strasbourg, in particular Ad van Loon, for support, as we would Christophe Poirel in the Council of Europe. We are particularly grateful also to the staff of the European Commission whom we interviewed in the course of our work.

The book has been written as a collaboration between the IMPS group in the School of Law at the University of Glasgow and the Programme in Comparative Media Law and Policy at the Centre for Socio-legal Studies in the University of Oxford. Further information on the work of both can be found on Websites at: <http://www.imps.gla.ac.uk> and at <http://www.vii. org/PCMLP>

David Goldberg, Tony Prosser, Stefaan Verhulst
Glasgow and Oxford
May 1998

General Editor's Preface

The Longman European Law Series is the first comprehensive series of topic-based books on EC Law aimed primarily at a student readership, though I have no doubt that they will also be found useful by academic colleagues and interested practitioners. It has become more and more difficult for a single course or a single book to deal comprehensively with all the major topics of Community law, and the intention of this series is to enable students and teachers to 'mix and match' topics which they find to be of interest; it may also be hoped that the publication of this Series will encourage the study of areas of Community law which have historically been neglected in degree courses. However, while the Series may have a student readership in mind, the authors have been encouraged to take an academic and critical approach, placing each topic in its overall Community context, and also in its socio-economic and political context where relevant.

This study of EC Media Law and Policy shows both the impact of basic EC Treaty rules on the European media industries and the development of an EC policy, notably in the area of broadcasting. Furthermore it sets the EC developments in a wider Europan context. While media law is hardly a matter of traditional legal study, it is a rapidly growing area with a huge economic impact, and an area where the EC itself has been in the forefront of developments. The series is particularly fortunate to have benefited in this book from a continuing collaboration between the authors which was developed in an ESRC-funded project on regulating the media.

John A. Usher

Table of Cases

Bond Van Adverteerders v The
Netherlands [1988] ECR 2085.
Case 352/85 **22**

Coditel v Ciné Vog [1980] 2 ECR
881. Case 62/79 **22, 47, 49, 50**

Commission v Belgium (Case
C-11/95) [1997] 2 CMLR 289 **70,
71**

Commission v United Kingdom (Case
C-222/94) [1996] 3CMLR 793 **70,
72**

De Haes and Gijsels v Belgium, no.
7/1996/626/809 **35**

Elliniki Radiophonia
Tiléorass-Anonimi Etairia v
Dimotiki Etairia Pliroforissis, Case
No C-260/89, 18 June 1991,
[1991] ECR 1–2925 **58**

*GETE Srl v Ministero delle Poste e
Telecommunicazioni (C-339/94) **73**

Holland Media Group (HMG), Case
Nr. IV/M.553, 20 September 1995
89

Informationsverein Lentia v Austria,
17 EHRR 93 **15**

Italian State v Saachi [1974] 1 ECR
409. Case 155/73 **1, 9, 13, 22, 49**

Jersild v Denmark, 23 September
1994, Series A vol. 298 **35**

Konsumentombudsmannen v De
Agostini Svenska Förlad AB and
TV-Shop I Sverige AB (Joined
Cases C-34, C-35 and C-36/95)
[1997] All ER (EC) 687 **74**

Leclerc-Siplec, Case C-412/93, [1995]
1 ECR 179 **69**

Marknadsföringslagen 1975: 1418
74

MSG Media Service, Case Nr
IV/M.469, 9 November 1994 **89**

Nordic Satellite Distribution, Case Nr
IV/M.490, 19 July 1995 **89**

Oberschlick No. 2 v Austria (1998)
25 EHRR 357 **35**

Otto-Preminger-Institut v Austria, 20
September 1994, Series A vol.
295-A.) **35**

Paul Denuit Case (Case C-14/96)
[1997] 3 CMLR 943 **72**

Procureur du Roi v Debauve [1980] 2
ECR 833. Case 52/79 **22, 47, 49,
57**

Radio ABC v Austria (1988) 25
EHRR 185 **35–6**

*Radio Italia Solo Musica Srl e.a.
(C-338/94) **73**

Radio Telefis Eireann (RTE) v
Independent Television C-241/91 P
and C242/91 P, 6 April 1995,
[1995] All ER (EC) 416 **88**

*Radio Torre (C-328/94) **73**

Rendez-Vous Télévision case, C(96)
3933 final **66**

*Rete A Srl (C-329/94) **73**

*Reti Televisive Italiane SpA (RTI)
(C-320/94) **73**

Rutili v Minister for the Interior
[1975] ECR 1219. Case 36/75 **47**

Telesystem Tirol Kabeltelevision
v Austria (1997) 24 EHRR CD
11 **35**

*Vallau Italiana Promomarket Srl. (C-337/94) **73**

Vereniging Weekblad Bluf! v the Netherlands, 9 February 1995, Series A vol. 306-A **35**

VT4 Case (Case C-56/96) [1997] 3 CMLR 1225 **72**

Wingrove v United Kingdom, No 19/1995/525/611) **35**

Worm v Austria (1998) 25 EHRR 454 **35**

*These are joined cases under [1997] 1 CMLR 346

Table of Directives

Directive 83/189/EEC, laying down a procedure for the provision of information in the fields of technical standards and regulations, OJ 1983 L 109. **103, 104**

Council Directive 84/450/EEC of 10 September 1984 on the approximation of the laws, regulations and administrative provisions of the Member States concerning misleading advertising, OJ 1997 L 290. **93**

Council Directive 86/529/EEC on the adoption of common technical specifications of the MAC/packet family of standards for direct satellite broadcasting, OJ 1986 L 311/28. **53**

Commission Directive 88/301/EEC of 16 May 1988 on competition in the markets in telecommunications equipment, OJ 1988 L 131/73. **76, 106**

Directive 89/337/EEC to promote HDTV, OJ 1989 L 142/1. **54**

Directive 89/552/EEC of 3 October 1989 on the cordination of certain provisions laid down by law, regulation or administrative action in Member States concerning the pursuit of television broadcasting activities, ('Television Without Frontiers Directive'), OJ 1989 L 298/23. **1, 6, 12, 15, 22, 56–75, 95, 122**

Council Directive 90/387/EEC, of 28 June 1990 on the establishment of the internal market for telecommunications services through the implementation of open network provision ('Open Framework Directive'), OJ 1990 L 192/1. **106, 107**

Commission Directive 90/388/EEC of 28 June 1990 on the liberalization of telecommunication services, OJ 1990 L 192/10. **77**

Council Directive of 14 May 1991 on the legal protection of computer programmes, OJ 1991 L 122/42. **87**

Council Directive 92/38/EEC of 11 May 1992 on the adoption of standards for satellite broadcasting of television signals OJ 1992 L 137/17. **54, 84**

Council Directive of 19 November 1992 on rental and lending rights related to copyright in the field of intellectual property, OJ 1992 L 346. **87**

Council Directive of 27 September 1993 on the coordination of certain rules concerning copyright and rights related to copyright applicable to satellite broadcasting and cable re-transmission, OJ 1993 L 248. **87**

Council Directive of 29 October 1993 harmonizing the term of protection of copyright and certain related rights. OJ 1993 L 290. **87**

Commission Directive 94/46/EC of 13 October 1994 amending Directive

88/301/EEC and Directive 90/388/EEC in regards to satellite communications, OJ 1994 L 268/15. **77**

Commission Directive 95/51/EC of 18 October 1995 amending Directive 90/388/EEC, regarding the restrictions on the use of cable television networks for the provision of already liberalized telecommunications services, OJ 1995 L 256/49. **77, 78**

Directive 95/46/EC of the European Parliament and of the Council of 24 October 1995 on the protection of individuals with regard to the processing of personal data and on the free movement of such data. OJ 1995 L 281/31. **117**

Directive 95/47/EC of the European Parliament and of the Council of 24 October 1995 on the use of standards for the transmission of television signals, OJ 1995 L 281/51. **85, 93**

Directive 95/62/EC on the application of the open network provision to voice telephony OJ 1995 L 321/6. **107**

Directive 96/9/EC of 11 March 1996 concerning the legal protection of databases, OJ 1996 L 77/20. **87**

Directive 96/16/EC on the liberalization of public voice telephony, OJ 1996 L 74/13. **78, 106**

Directive 97/13/EC of April 1997 on licensing ('Licensing Directive'), OJ 1997 L 117/15. **77**

Parliament and Council Directive 97/36/EC of 30 June 1997, amending Directive 89/552/EC, OJ 1997 L 202/60. **59**

Parliament and Council Directive 97/55/EC of 6 October 1997, amending Directive 84/450/EEC so as to include comparative advertising, OJ 1997 L 290. **93–4**

Table of Web Sites

Audio-visual EUREKA –
    <*http://www.aveureka.be*>

Council of Europe –
    <*http://www.coe.fr*>

Directorate of Human Rights –
    <*http://www.dhdirhr.coe.int*>

EURIMAGES – <*http://culture.coe.int*>

European Audio-visual Observatory –
    <*http://www.coe.int*>

European Broadcasting Union –
    <*http://www.ebu.ch*>

European Radiocommunications
    Office – <*http://www.ero.dk*>

European Union –
    <*http://www.europa.eu.int*>

IM (Information Market) Europe –
    <*http://www2.echo.lu/home.html*>

IMP – University of Glasgow –
    <*http://www.imps.gla.ac.uk*>

Information Society Project Office –
    <*http://www.ispo.cec.be*>

MEDIA II – <*http://europa.eu.int/en/
    comm/dg10/avpolicy/media/en/
    home-m2.html*>

Programme in Comparative Media
    Law & Policy –
    <*http://www.vii.org/ PCMLP* >

Abbreviations

ACTS	Advanced Communications Technologies and Services
AVE	Audio-visual Eureka
CEPT	European Conference of Postal and Telecommunications Administrations
DG	Directorate-General
DSI	Detailed Spectrum Investigations
DVB	Digital Video Broadcasting
EBU	European Broadcasting Union
ECJ	European Court of Justice
ECOSOC	Economic and Social Committee
ECPs	European Common Proposals
EEA	European Economic Area
EFCA	European Film Companies Alliance
EGTA	European Group of Television Advertising
EIF	European Investment Fund
EIM	European Institute for the Media
EP	European Parliament
EPRA	European Platform of Regulatory Authorities
ERC	European Radiocommunications Committee
ERO	European Radiocommunications Office
ETSI	European Telecommunications Standards Institute
GATT	General Agreement on Tariffs and Trade
HDTV	High Definition Television
HLEG	High Level Expert Group
IBC	Integrated Broadband Communication
ICT	Information and Communication Technologies
ISAD	International Conference on Information Society and Development
ITU	International Telecommunications Union
MEDIA	Measures to Encourage the Development of the Industry of Audio-visual Production

MFN	Most-favoured Nation
MLIS	Multilingual Information Society
OIRT	International Radio and Television Organization
ONP	Open Network Provision
OSCE	Organization for Security and Cooperation in Europe
PSB	Public Service Broadcasting
SME	Small- and Medium-sized Enterprises
WIPO	World Intellectual Property Organization
WTO	World Trade Organization

Table of Equivalence after Treaty of Amsterdam

Treaty establishing the European Community *(Treaty of Rome)*	New Numbering
Article 3	Article 3
Article 3a	Article 4
Article 3b	Article 5
Article 3c	Article 6
Article 4	Article 7
Article 7d	Article 16
Article 9	Article 23
Article 12	Article 25
Article 30	Article 28
Article 31	Repealed
Article 48	Article 39
Article 52	Article 43
Article 56	Article 46
Article 57	Article 47
Article 59	Article 49
Article 62	Repealed
Article 66	Article 55
Article 85	Article 81
Article 86	Article 82
Article 90	Article 86
Article 92	Article 97
Article 100	Article 94
Article 127	Article 150
Article 128	Article 151
Article 130	Article 157
Article 189b	Article 251
Article 222	Article 295
Article 235	Article 308

CHAPTER ONE

Introduction

The European media industries form a peculiarly complex object for legal regulation. Thus the media are ostensibly similar to other types of economic service and indeed the media industries are among the most dynamic and influential of all European businesses. Indeed, at the earliest stage of Community interest in media regulation the Court of Justice confirmed that the media fall within the provisions of the Treaty concerned with free movement of services.[1] Thus one strong theme of Community media law and policy has been liberalization through removing barriers to freedom of transmission and of reception within the European Union. This has been true of the conventional media, notably broadcasting, and such lifting of barriers was a central theme of the *Television Without Frontiers* Directive[2] which forms the core of Community law directed specifically at the media and which will be discussed in detail in a later chapter. It is also true of a major industry which is becoming more and more closely linked to the media; that of telecommunications. Here the process of liberalization was based on strong action by the European Commission and culminated in the removal of restrictions on the provision of voice telecommunication services (in other words, sending speech rather than data) from the beginning of 1998. It is probably the most successful example of sustained Community action to open up an area previously dominated by national monopolies. The theme of freedom to provide services is also an important one in relation to the so-called 'new media', of which digital television and the Internet are likely to become the most important. As we shall see, the Community took action aimed at grasping the implications of

[1]. *Italian State v Saachi* [1974] 1 ECR 409. Case 155/73.
[2]. Directive 89/552/EEC, OJ L 298/23, 17.10.89.

I

these developments well before this was done by most national governments. How to develop an open 'information society' has become the subject of debates central to Community media policy.

Similarly, Community competition law based on arts 85 and 86 of the Treaty of Rome and on the Mergers Regulation[3] has also become of increasing importance and will be crucial in relation to the 'new media' as markets are opened up but commercial pressures lead to mergers and the seeking of market advantage by anticompetitive means. Important steps have already been taken, for example, to ensure that the market for the special equipment necessary for the reception of digital broadcasts will not be controlled by the owner of one form of technology. Competition law shares the assumption which underlies policy on the freedom to provide services that the media offer commodities, and so are subject to the same types of regulation as that applying to other industries. The underlying aim is that of maintaining open markets within which consumers can exercise their sovereignty.

We shall also document a number of ways in which the Community has attempted to increase the competitiveness of the European media industries through various programmes, including the provision of finance, supporting training and encouraging the growth of common standards. This can be seen as falling within the traditional field of industrial policy and, like much other such policy, has been of uneven value with some notable failures such as early attempts to develop a format for High Definition Television. Again it does not at first sight seem to involve a very different set of activities from that which is applied to other industries producing products other than information and entertainment.

However, as was noted early on in debates over Community competence, the media and its products are not like pigmeat or banking services. They carry the baggage of forming part of our culture, of being perceived as having moral implications, of being associated with concepts of public service and, finally, of being the object of important rights set out in national and international instruments. Thus, a theme throughout the history of Community media policy has been that the media have a cultural dimension. Early on, this was conceived as part of the means by which the Member States could be integrated into a unified Community

---

[3]. Council Regulation 4064/89 on the control of concentrations; OJ 1990 L257/14.

2

through consciousness of a common culture, e.g. through the provision of a Community television channel. More recently, the assumption that one goal of the Community should be to protect
European (especially French) culture and language against the all-
conquering US cultural world lay behind the serious dispute concerning quotas for European programmes which arose in the
GATT negotiations. This cultural question is also of importance in
determining questions of Community competence, as we shall see.
Although the amendments to the Treaty under the Maastricht
Treaty of 1991 did include an important reference to cultural matters, this is limited in important ways and does not permit the use
of full Community lawmaking powers to harmonise laws of the
Member States.[4]

A further dimension of the media is not entirely unrelated to
this cultural concern; this is that the products of the media are perceived as having important moral dimensions. Thus public debate
on the media often seems dominated by fears of the effects of the
portrayal of sex and violence, a concern which affects the question
of freedom to transmit programmes and the nature of their content. Again, this concern is likely to increase rather than decrease
with the development of new types of service such as digital satellite television permitting an enormous increase in channels available
and with an increasing ability to penetrate national boundaries
through the extended coverage of satellite 'footprints'. Indeed, one
issue faced by the UK Government and on which action has already been taken, has been the extent to which Community law
permits action to be taken to prevent the receipt of such services
originating in another Member State. The growth of the Internet is
already posing further problems, in particular in relation to the involvement of children in pornographic content. Rather than the
media industries providing a mere service, then, they are often perceived as playing a major role in shaping public and private morality, and one important question has been the extent to which
exceptions to freedom of movement of services can reflect this.

If the aspects of the media relating to public morality seem
highly unusual in the context of the provision of services in the
Community, a more familiar question is that of the role of the
media as a public service. During the 1990s there has been extensive debate within the Community on the degree to which liberali-

---

4. See Article 128 of the Treaty as inserted by the *Treaty of European Union*.

zation, especially telecommunications liberalization where there is a strong impetus from the Commission behind it, is threatening the ability of public services to operate and to act as a source of social solidarity rather than simply competing in the consumer market-place.[5] This debate will result in some minor changes to the Treaty as a result of the Treaty of Amsterdam.[6] The debate on the role of public service, and more specifically public service broadcasting, has also been intense in the media field where such broadcasting has often been perceived as central to Member States' cultural and political identities. Here also minor changes are included in the Amsterdam Treaty.[7] It is doubtful if they will change very much either in legal or in practical terms, but they are nevertheless important in suggesting that the dimension of public service is one important way in which the older media, if not the newer, differ from most commodities traded in the European Union. Moreover, recent action to permit Member States to prevent the broadcasting of key sporting events only on subscription services, represents a concern to protect traditions of universal access to broadcast material, and universal service has been a central element in the liberalization of telecommunications in the European Union; it is now also an important element in the Green Paper on media convergence.

Finally, a further dimension which exists in relation to the media is that of the importance of human rights, notably the right to freedom of expression and the right to privacy. Both of these are of course protected (subject to the inevitable exceptions) under the European Convention on Human Rights, and art. 10 in particular of the Convention has had a key role in relation to Community media policy. Indeed, it could be said that this has supplied the basic constitutional principles for media policy, in a way which has been done by decisions of constitutional courts in a number of member states.[8] We shall not be able to assess the role of human rights in general in Community law in this work, but it will be

---

5. For an account of the principles applying in Community Law and of the resulting tensions see Scott, C., *Competition and Coordination: Their Role in the Future of European Community Telecommunications Regulation*, Centre for the Study of Regulated Industries, 1995, and for the views of the Commission before the Amsterdam summit see *Communication on Services of General Interest in Europe* (1996).
6. *Treaty of Amsterdam*, inserting a new art. 7d into the EC Treaty.
7. *Ibid.*, Protocol on the System of Public Broadcasting in the Member States.
8. For the role of constitutional courts in relation to broadcasting see Craufurd Smith, R., *Broadcasting Law and Fundamental Rights*, Clarendon, 1997.

necessary to include coverage of the larger European dimension including the Convention. Indeed, we shall also refer to other activities of the Council of Europe as it has undertaken extensive work on media law and regulation, notably through its Convention on Transfrontier Television.[9]

The media, then, are significantly different from other services which are the subject of Community law and regulation. Added complexity is created by the fact that there has also been institutional conflict within the Community with different rationales for regulation being adopted by different institutional actors. It should also be stressed that there is considerable variety in the types of media which are covered. Most Community action has concerned broadcasting. Traditionally this has taken the form of public service broadcasting in which only a limited number of channels is available, due both to technical restrictions of spectrum scarcity and to government policy favouring restriction on the provision of services to protect the public service channels. This is already well into a process of fundamental change, initially through the development of cable and satellite delivery and more recently through the convergence of broadcasting, telecommunications and computer technologies to produce the so-called 'new media' including digital television and the Internet. These promise both a new abundance of channels and vastly increased consumer control over content; indeed, it could be argued that they will replace the traditional forms of public service broadcasting by markets in which consumers are sovereign and content regulation will become no more important than it has been in relation to the content of phone calls. The social implications of these developments will also be profound. To its credit, the Community and especially the Commission appreciated the importance of these developments well before most national governments and extensive discussions of their implications have occurred within the Community, although the future direction of policy remains somewhat unclear. We shall return to the question of whether these market developments will make Community regulation unnecessary in the final chapter.

It will be helpful at this point to give a brief outline of the scheme of this book. We commence with a discussion of the differ-

---

9. *European Treaty Series* (1989) no. 132.

5

ent rationales which have underlain Community policy in relation to the media; as is already evident, these are unusually complex and potentially conflicting. This leads to discussion of the very closely related question of Community competence to take action in this field where the relationship between liberalisation of the movement of services and cultural concerns has provoked considerable tension; we also discuss the provisions of the Treaty on which Community action has been based. However, it is misleading to think of the Community as a monolithic policy-maker and institutional conflict has also been apparent with different rationales for intervention being associated with different institutions, so a brief discussion of the relevant institutions will be provided. Finally in this section, the pan-European context, especially the role of the Council of Europe, is discussed because of its central importance in shaping Community policy.

In Chapter Four we deal with the origins of Community media policy, beginning with early attempts by the Parliament to develop the media as a means of integration, but concentrating on the Green Paper of 1984 and its background; this provided the first coherent attempt at a Community media policy.[10] We also include in this chapter a discussion of the origins of Community support for the media industries and technical programmes. Whilst these were somewhat different in focus from the legal and regulatory action proposed in the Green Paper, they are of importance in showing media policy as a whole and in context.

Chapter Five is in many ways the heart of this book. It contains an exhaustive discussion of the 1989 Directive *Television Without Frontiers*, still the central element in Community policy in relation to broadcast media.[11] There is also analysis of the 1997 revisions to the Directive, and the body of caselaw from the Court of Justice interpreting the Directive. The next chapter describes other legal measures and the later history of support programmes for the media industries, and attempts to encourage technological innovation through standardization including the ill-fated attempts to support the development of High Definition Television. Attempts at reforming copyright law are also described as is the role of competition policy, especially in relation to media ownership where progress has so far been limited. This central section of the book

---

10. COM (84) 300 (final).
11. Directive 89/552/EEC, OJ L 298/23, 17.10.89.

should thus provide a comprehensive account of Community policy towards the broadcasting media.

As anticipated above, however, we are in a process of what is
often claimed to be revolutionary change in the media, with claims
that we are on the verge of an 'information society' as a result of
the convergence of the older media with telecommunications and
with computing. The Community deserves credit for realising the
potential of this change before many national governments did so,
and Chapter Seven describes the extensive debates which have occurred around the information society concept and its future, as
well as summarizing the extensive, and successful, measures taken
to liberalize telecommunications throughout the Union, an essential basis for other information policies. The 1997 Green Paper[12]
on convergence is discussed, and the chapter concludes by dealing
with policies on data protection which return us to our earlier concerns with the relationship between Community policy and the
European Convention on Human Rights. The book concludes with
a brief chapter bringing the themes together and attempting to
assess the future of Community media policy.

12. COM (97)623, 3 December 1997.

CHAPTER TWO

Foundations of European Community media policy

Introduction and policy rationales[1]

This chapter deals with a variety of themes, events and mechanisms. The main, though not exclusive, focus is on the origins of audio-visual policy in the European Community.[2] Moreover the term 'media' is *principally* understood in Europe to mean audio-visual broadcasting, partly as a result of the strong lobbying of broadcasting associations such as the European Broadcasting Union (EBU – see page 39). However, it cannot be denied that television and video dominate the entertainment scene in Europe and as such play an important strategic economic and social role.[3] Thus to refer to audio-visual policy is almost certainly to refer to

---

1. See Collins R., *Broadcasting and Audiovisual Policy in the European Single Market,* John Libbey, 1994; Maggiore M., *Audiovisual Production in the Single Market*, CEC, 1990; Schwartz I., 'Broadcasting Without Frontiers in the European Community' 6(1) *Journal of Media Law and Practice* (1985) 26 and 'Broadcasting and the EEC Treaty' 11 *European Law Review* (1986) pp. 7–60; Wallace R. and Goldberg D. 'The EEC Directive on Television Broadcasting' 9 *Yearbook of European Law* (1989) pp. 175, 175–178; and Wallace R. and Goldberg D., 'Television Broadcasting: The Community's Response' *Common Market Law Review* 26: (1989) 717–728; Wallace R. and Goldberg D., *Regulating the Audiovisual Industry: the Second Phase*, Butterworths, London, 1991; Humphreys P.J., *Mass Media and Media Policy in Western Europe*, Manchester University Press, 1996, pp. 257–296.

2. Though the term 'European Union' has been introduced into the European lexicon by the Treaty of Maastricht or the European Union Treaty, the references in this book will largely be to the European Community (EC). This is the legally correct term for European Economic Community established by the Treaty of Rome or EC Treaty. European Union properly describes the whole complex of activities envisaged by the Maastricht Treaty, that is to say the new areas of political cooperation which fall outside the competence of the institutions of the Community. Separation of 'Community' elements from 'Union' elements in European policy is certainly not watertight, but these problems are irrelevant here.

3. See for instance *Audio-visual Statistics – Report 1995.* (Eurostat).

policies which will have an impact on TV broadcasting. However, the issue of terminology can still cause problems. One author has noted that 'The audio-visual sector in the EC will usually refer to TV and film activities. Reference to media will be more likely, in the EC context, to refer to TV broadcasting (and when considering media ownership, also to radio broadcasting and the press)'.[4] However, with the growth towards an 'information society' it has also been suggested that 'The audio-visual sector which covers programme production and distribution ("software"), to which equipment manufacturing ("hardware") can be added, has an economic importance that is often underestimated as compared to its unquestionable cultural significance.'[5] The latter field will also be covered in this book.

During the first 25 years of its existence the European Community did not develop a comprehensive and integrated media or audio-visual policy. Early attempts at pan-European broadcasting integration were instigated not by the European Commission but by independent organizations (e.g. EBU) and individual member states. The evolution of the European Community's audio-visual policy and regulation only got under way in the early nineteen-eighties although the aims of that policy have been rather consistent: ' to create a genuine European audio-visual area and make it work; [and] to implement a strategy for strengthening European audio-visual production industries'.[6] Apart from early policy development, it is, however worth remembering that the European Court of Justice decided several cases involving audio-visual issues even before that time. The most notable, perhaps, is the judgment in *Italian State v Saachi*[7] which was utilized by the EC to justify its regulation of broadcasting. Other, slightly later, cases dealt with national restrictions on television undertakings in the light of competition rules, Member States' ability to restrict the freedom to advertise, and copyright protection and re-transmitted programmes.

4. Hitchens, L., 'Identifying European Community Audio-visual Policy in the Dawn of the Information Society', 2 *Yearbook of Media and Entertainment Law* (1996) 45.
5. *White Paper on growth, competitiveness, and employment – The challenges and ways forward into the 21st century*, COM(93) 700 final Brussels, 5 December 1993; C – The Audiovisual Sector, 5.10 Introduction; available also at; <http://www.ispo.cec.be/infosoc/backg/whitpaper/ch5c_1.html>
6. Memo from Mr Oreja to the Commission *Audiovisual policy : progress and prospects* <http://europa.eu.int/en/comm/dg10/avpolicy/key_doc/orejcome.html>
7. [1974] 1 ECR 409. Case 155/73.

Initially, the main policy driver was the European Parliament, followed by the Commission. In general, two distinct phases of policy evolution linked with different rationales can be identified.

At first (1981–1984), the rationale was that media (and television in particular) would be the means by which a European identity and citizenship could be forged. The dissemination of European information by European public TV and the watching of television programmes in common would, it was hoped, create and foster a sense of being 'European' and thus European unity.[8] This was a political, rather than an economic (or even cultural) rationale for regulation.[9] This political approach was treated somewhat sceptically by broadcasters. As early as 1950, European public service broadcasters had set up the European Broadcasting Union (as the successor to the International Broadcasting Union) to facilitate solutions to common legal and technical problems and to exchange news and other programmes (see below). During the 1930s, there had already been a significant traffic in cross-border transmissions of radio programmes from such organizations as CLR (Luxemburg) and Radio Normandie. However this concept of 'cultural unity' changed rather quickly towards a more realistic concern about how to preserve Europe's existing 'cultural diversity'[10] and by 1984–85, the view became that the audio-visual sector was of fundamental importance in completing the internal market.[11] The aims were twofold. The first was to respond to the growing market in satellite and cable (re)transmissions which required liberalization and freedom from national restrictions and so 'To ensure that all residents in the EC have access to all EC broadcasts which have become possible with satellite and cable technology.'[12] The second was to create a European common market in production and distribution which could challenge the United States (or *le défi américain*[13]) in economies of scale.

8. For a discussion on the role of the media in unifying the citizens of Europe see Weymouth T. and Lmizet B., (eds), *Markets and Myths: Forces for Change in the European Media*, Addison Wesley Longman, 1997.
9. Schlesinger P., From cultural defence to political cultures: media, politics and collective identity in the European Union, 19 *Media Culture and Society* (1997) 369–91.
10. Collins R., footnote 1 on p. 8.
11. Document 7674/85: *Commission Communication to the Council on completing the internal market; White Paper Completing the Internal Market* COM (85) 310 final points 115–117 and Annex timetable 27.
12. <http://europa.eu.int/comm/sg/scadplus/leg/en/lvb/l24101.htm>
13. See Servan-Schreiber J., *Le Défi Américain – The American Challenge*, Penguin, 1968.

Finally, it should not be forgotten that audio-visual services (including broadcasting and, in particular, communications) are included as one of the 'services of general interest in Europe' whereby, 'television and radio have a general interest dimension, despite the structural and technological changes affecting these markets. The general interest considerations basically concern the content of broadcasts, being linked to moral and democratic values, such as pluralism, information ethics and protection of the individual.[14] This means that policy has been influenced by broader debates, right up to the 1997 Amsterdam Treaty, concerning the role of public services within the European Union, as we shall indicate below.[15] Moreover, this approach has also led to major disputes about the competence of the European Community in this field. As a result the EC has been obliged to avoid a cultural definition of audio-visual products and insists instead on a strictly economic definition. As Jacques Delors declared in 1985: 'Under the Treaty of Rome, the EC does not have the means to impose a cultural policy. It will therefore have to tackle the problem from an economic point of view'[16] This chapter will now consider issues of competence in greater detail.

The competence issue

The legal framework and the competences of the European Community are determined by the *Treaty of Rome* (the EC Treaty) as amended, which is, in effect, the constitution of the European Community. The principal treaties amending the EC Treaty are the *Single European Act*, the *Treaty on European Union* (Maastricht Treaty) and the recent *Treaty of Amsterdam*. The European Community can only act when, and if, there is a sufficient legal basis for action contained in the Treaties. Moreover, there is a clear hierarchical structure between the Treaties and Community acts in the form of regulations, directives and decisions. All acts adopted by the institutions must comply with the provisions of the Treaties.

Not all Member States were agreed, or convinced, that the

14. European Commission, *Services of General Interest in Europe*. Brussels: COM (96)443 final, 11 September 1996.
15. For a discussion see Verhulst S., Public Service Broadcasting in Europe. In: *Utilities Law Review*, 8(2) March–April, 1997, pp. 31–3.
16. Quoted in Negrine R. and Papthanassopoulos S., *The Internationalisation of Television*, Pinter, 1990, p. 57.

European Community even had competence to regulate the media. Broadcasters and others in Member States considered audio-visual services, such as broadcasting, part of 'culture' – which was not contained in the Treaty of Rome. The question asked was, how could the Community justify its involvement in this area, and was it not intruding in a non-economic area? The UK and Denmark, in particular, were not happy about this apparent extension of Community activity to cultural matters; and, to a lesser extent, their view was shared by Germany and Belgium.

The Commission's Green Paper on the establishment of the common market for broadcasting issued in 1984[17] (to be discussed fully below) considered in some detail the case for the Community's involvement in the area of national broadcasting policy. The problem was referred to in two reports by the House of Lords Select Committee on the European Communities.[18] The Committee noted that, 'The Commission had to prove that Community action was needed to regulate any aspects of broadcasting because they directly affected the functioning of the Common Market, bearing in mind that neither the advancement of cultural activities nor their control is harming the objectives of the Community as laid down in the Treaty.'[19] Furthermore, the Committee recalled the words of the Legal Affairs Committee that 'no provision at all is made in the Treaties of Rome as regards policy relating to the media'.[20]

The Commission put forward several arguments to justify its competence:

- the Commission had been requested by the Parliament to prepare rules to facilitate European broadcasting to foster European unity – indeed it has a moral/political right to act since broadcasting (which is a technique for disseminating information) is relevant for European integration;
- although broadcasting might be a cultural service, it, nonetheless, is carried out for remuneration – thus it is also an economic activity;

[17.] COM (84) 300 final.
[18.] *Television Without Frontiers*, Select Committee on the European Communities (HL 43, 1985–86); *European Broadcasting*, Select Committee on the European Communities (HL 67, 1986–87) Part 3.
[19.] *Ibid.*, HL 67, para. 11.
[20.] quoted from Doc. PE.74.394 of 1980 in *ibid.* p. 14.

- under the Treaty arts 57(2) and 66, the Community had a duty to remove the barriers to Member States' freedom to provide broadcasting services and the Community is the most appropriate body for this work as opposed to any other national, regional or global entity.

The Select Committee was dismissive of the 'insubstantial' argument from integration, believing the Commission treated broadcasting primarily as an economic activity and not a cultural one which alone would have lent weight to its claim. It regarded as contradictory the claim that the common market in broadcasting would enhance the common market in distribution as the 'practical effect of the Green Paper will be to encourage the very broadcasters (namely satellite television channels) who use the greatest proportion of cheap bought-in material, mainly from the USA'.[21]

The Green Paper states that 'the EEC Treaty applies not only to economic activities but, as a rule, also to all activities carried out for remuneration, regardless of whether they take place in the economic, social, cultural (including in particular information, creative, or artistic activities and entertainment) sporting or any other sphere'.[22] Accordingly, the Commission believed it had the right and duty to act in this area, supporting its stance with the opinion of the European Court of Justice in the *Saachi* decision (above) that the transmission of television signals involves the Treaty rules on the freedom to provide services. Much of the evidence that the Select Committee received was highly critical of this view. For example, witnesses stated, *inter alia*, that the *Saachi* case dealt with advertising and cable and, thus, was not about general broadcasting as such; that broadcasting is in its nature different from 'cross-frontier traffic in pig-meat or banking'; that broadcasting is 'predominantly not an economic service but an important aspect of the cultural and political life in the widest terms'; that national broadcasting upholds the very identity and existence of a country; and that (as regards public service broadcasting in particular), remuneration, whilst an essential prerequisite for making programmes, is not the purpose for which they are made. The Select Committee considered that 'The difference in approach between the Commission's critics and the Commission may be summed up as the difference between a traditional view that information is largely a social-cultural resource and a newer market-orientated

21. HL 43, *op. cit.*, p .14.   22. Green Paper, *op. cit.*, p. 6.

view that it is just another commodity to be bought and sold'.[23] The implications of this difference in view continue to echo in current debates surrounding broadcasting in the European Union.

Interestingly, in the light of the impetus for European-level action proposed by the Parliament (EP), which will be discussed in more detail below, the EP also contested this economistic understanding of broadcasting. Although art. 100 of the Treaty on approximation of laws was considered to justify Community action, the Legal Affairs Committee of the EP dissented from that view, stating that broadcasting was a cultural matter requiring diversity and the protection of vulnerable persons. The Legal Affairs Committee's preferred basis was art. 235 providing a more general basis for action necessary to attain Community objectives.

In the view of the House of Lords Committee, adoption by the Commission of this approach would have avoided much criticism as it would have 'required the Commission to develop an overall media policy . . . and [to take] fuller account of cultural, social and political as well as economic issues . . .'.[24] The Committee concluded that the EP had failed to make the general case that all aspects of broadcasting were within the scope of the Treaty; cable retransmissions were clearly within its remit, composition of programmes was not.

The European Commission's own view, as expressed to the Committee, was that 'the opening up of the audio-visual industry is a central part of the Community's commitment to completing the internal market by 1992'.[25] The tart response from the Committee was 'The question arises whether broadcasting can be regarded as an essential element in the functioning of the common market'. As for the approach of the Commission that it must facilitate the removal of barriers to freedom to provide services, including broadcasting, the liberalization proposals fitted this rationale but there were also unwelcome restrictions and obligations such as quotas which the Commission argued it must develop to make the outcome of liberalization fair, and these went beyond what was required by simple removal of barriers.

As regards the detail of the Commission's competence, witnesses to the House of Lords Committee were sceptical, at best, concerning:

---

[23]. HL 43, *op. cit.*, para. 37.   [24]. *ibid.* para 38.
[25]. HL 67, *op. cit.* para 13.

- quotas for European programming (which were not included in the Green Paper, but announced by the Commission during the Committee's inquiry);
- the amount of time to be permitted for advertising;
- rules regarding tobacco and alcohol advertising;
- the protection of young people; and
- copyright protection.

The general conclusion was that the Select Committee ' . . . continues to question the competence of the Community to act in some of the areas . . . since the Community is competent only in so far as broadcasting directly affects the functioning of the common market' and that ' . . . even if it were within the competence of the Community to regulate most aspects of broadcasting, it would still be a matter of political choice for the Member States whether they wished to leave these fields unregulated and within the discretion of Member States or preferred to have Community legislation on them . . . '.[26]

Foundation texts

As already noted in the section on competence above, the European Community's involvement in the audio-visual sector was largely premised on the opinion of the Court in the *Saachi* case that the transmission of television signals constitutes a service, and, thus, broadcasting, *inter alia,* comes within the scope of the Articles on freedom of movement of services. The Green Paper (and the first version of the Directive *Television Without Frontiers* to be discussed in Chapter Five below) used the general approximation powers under art 100 on which to base proposals for harmonization. An important account of this process has been provided by Ivo Schwartz, then Director with responsibility for approximation of laws, freedom of establishment and freedom to provide services. He wrote that, apart from the general applicability of the EEC Treaty to cultural activities ('. . . activities carried out for remuneration, regardless of whether they take place in the economic, social, cultural (including in particular information, creative or artistic activities and entertainment) . . . or any other

26. HL 43 para 39.

15

sphere'), the 'EEC Treaty encompasses broadcasting in a multitude of ways . . . '.[27] In particular, he argued, the Treaty applies to:

- signals transmitted or relayed by radio, considering them to be services (art. 60). The Treaty provides for the abolition of restrictions and the prevention of any new restrictions on the freedom to provide broadcasting within the Community (arts 59 and 62). Thus broadcasters may transmit their signals to other Member States ('freedom of Community-wide broadcasting'), recipients in Member States may 'capture such signals' (freedom of 'Community-wide broadcasting reception') and recipients may include signals 'in their own selection of broadcasting' ('freedom of Community-wide choice of transmissions');
- 'broadcasters in their capacity as persons carrying on a self-employed activity for remuneration' (art. 52);
- 'national broadcasting and telecommunications legislation as the sum of the provisions laid down in individual Member States concerning the taking up and pursuit of self-employed activity, *viz.* broadcasting' (art. 57(2));
- workers in broadcasting organizations, who are guaranteed freedom of movement (art. 48) and those working for broadcasters in a self-employed capacity (to whom the Treaty offers freedom to provide cross-frontier services and freedom of establishment (arts 52 and 59)). 'In so doing, it extends the freedom of reporting, expressing opinions and presenting cultural performances to the entire territory of the Community';
- those 'technical provisions governing broadcasting (relay procedures and equipment, transmitters, receivers, standardization etc.) as directly affect the establishment or functioning of the common market' (art. 100);
- broadcasters 'as undertakings that deal in materials, sound recordings, films and other products which they need to carry on their activity'. These activities are guaranteed by the provisions on the freedom of movement of goods between Member States (arts 9, 12, 30 and 31);
- broadcasters 'in their capacity as undertakings, engaged in competition' (arts 85 and 86).

[27.] Schwartz I., Broadcasting and the EEC Treaty, *op. cit.*

More recently, the European Union's own overview of European Audio-visual Policy includes a section on 'Rules and Procedures'.[28] It describes the bases of the Treaty's applicability to audio-visual policy thus:

> the Treaty contains a large number of articles relevant to the audio-visual policy including 9, 12, 30 and 31 (free movement of goods) and 48 to 66 (freedom of movement of workers, right of establishment and freedom to provide services). In addition art. 127 provides for professional training projects, art 128 for promoting culture and art 130 for industrial policy initiatives. Competition rules and common commercial policy also play a significant role in this sector.

The reference to art. 128 is a reference to Title IX or the so-called 'culture article' of the Treaty of European Union of 1992. This is worth quoting in full and provides that:

1. The Community shall contribute to the flowering of the cultures of the Member States, while respecting their national and regional diversity and at the same time bringing the common cultural heritage to the fore.

2. Action by the Community shall be aimed at encouraging cooperation between Member States and, if necessary, supporting and supplementing their action in the following areas:
   – improvement of the knowledge and dissemination of the culture and history of the European peoples;
   – conservation and safeguarding of cultural heritage of European significance;
   – non-commercial cultural exchanges;
   – artistic and literary creation, including in the audio-visual sector.

3. The Community and the Member States shall foster cooperation with third countries and the competent international organizations in the sphere of culture, in particular the Council of Europe.

4. The Community shall take cultural aspects into account in its action under other provisions of this Treaty.

5. In order to contribute to the achievement of the objectives referred to in this Article, the Council:
   – acting in accordance with the procedure referred to in

---

28. <http://www.europa.eu.int/pol/av/en/info.htm#c2>

art. 189b and after consulting the Committee of the
Regions, shall adopt incentive measures, excluding any
harmonization of the laws and regulations of the Member
States. The Council shall act unanimously throughout the
procedures referred to in art. 189b;
– acting unanimously on a proposal from the Commission,
shall adopt recommendations.

The inclusion of this article is significant, particularly in the
light of the fact that early disagreements over the competence of
the Community to legislate for the audio-visual sector were precisely based on the view that the Community had no competence
over a sector that is, arguably, not economic or not wholly economic in the way other commodities are. The inclusion of 'Culture'
in the Treaty on European Union was part of a strategy 'to more
closely involve the people of Europe in the process of European integration'.[29] Historically, moves to integration 'have . . . been
economic and commercial, but now the aim is to take it further
from a broader base that could involve citizens to a greater degree
and strengthen the feeling of belonging to the European Union.' It
appears as if, without losing the liberalization approach, another
Community rationale is being overlaid on it which, in an apparent-
ly unconscious irony, echoes the sentiments and view of the earliest phase of interest for regulating information policy as expressed
by European Parliamentarians. However its scope remains very
limited. As can be seen above, the text of the article confines the
competence in the audio-visual field to 'artistic and literary creation, including in the audio-visual sector' rather than opening the
whole of the audio-visual sector to Community intervention. Further, it provides that the Council 'shall adopt incentive measures,
excluding any harmonization of the laws and regulations of the
Member States', which means the unavailability of 'hard law'.[30]
Therefore, the European Community is more or less limited to the
establishment of financial incentives in the area of culture. Moreover, Council decisions in cultural matters are to be taken unanimously rather than by qualified majority voting. These provisions

29. European union policies: culture : Current Position and Outlook
<http://www.europa.eu.int/comm/sg/scadplus/leg/en/s20014.htm> the following
quotes are from the same source.
30. See, Weatherill, S., *Law and the Integration in the European Union*, Clarendon,
1995, pp. 173–4.

can be seen as a significant success for the more liberal Member States (with the UK as the most pronounced example).

Other changes to the Treaty of Rome after the Treaty on European Union include in art. 3 establishing as one of the objectives of Community action 'a contribution to education and training of quality and to the flowering of the cultures of the Member States' and art. 92(3)(d) which stipulates that 'aid to promote culture and heritage conservation where such aid does not affect trading conditions and competition in the Community to an extent that is contrary to the common interest' can be considered compatible with the internal market (see below).

Clearly, not all the aims or fields of intervention are directly applicable to the audio-visual sector – or to broadcasting alone. Article 128 is the most pertinent, for as noted above the audio-visual area is specifically referred to as one of the areas for Community action. The relationship between culture generally and the audio-visual sector is also highlighted in the Commission's *First Report on the Consideration of Cultural Aspects in European Community Action*,[31] where the two objectives of the Community's audio-visual policy (setting-up and ensuring the functioning of a genuine European area for audio-visual services and implementing a strategy to reinforce the European programme industry) are 'being pursued by taking full account of the cultural dimension of the audio-visual sector'.

Finally, the 1997 Amsterdam Treaty amending the Treaty on European Union includes the following *Protocol on the System of Public Broadcasting in the Member States*:

> The provisions of the Treaty establishing the European Community shall be without prejudice to the competence of Member States to provide for the funding of public service broadcasting insofar as such funding is granted to broadcasting organisations for the fulfillment of the public service remit as conferred, defined and organised by each Member State, and insofar as such funding does not affect trading conditions and competition in the Community to an extent which would be contrary to the common interest, while the realisation of the remit of that public service shall be taken into account.

31. COM (96) 160; <http://www.europa.eu.int/en/comm/dg10/culture/cult-asp/en/part3/chap1.html>

It is not entirely surprising that this Protocol is in the Treaty as there has been lobbying over a number of years to protect and promote public service broadcasting in Europe, despite active opposition to aspects of the campaign by the Association of Commercial Television. In 1993, a Conference was held under the auspices of the European Broadcasting Union with the support of the MEDIA project (see below) which produced the Declaration 'Public Service Broadcasting: Europe's Opportunity'.[32] Even more influential was the adoption by the European Parliament on 17 September 1996 of the Resolution[33] on the role of public service television in the multi-media society based upon the 'Tongue Report'.[34]

The report starts from the assumption that public service broadcasting (PSB) is 'a foundation stone of a healthy interactive democratic society'. Moreover within the context of Europe, 'PSB has a responsibility to facilitate mutual knowledge and understanding between Europeans upon which European citizenship, key to European democracy can develop'. There had also been a lengthy debate on the role of public services within the European Union which had covered considerably wider territory than that of broadcasting alone.[35] It is however unclear what effect, if any, the new protocol will have in practice.

The European institutions, their interests and their impact

The Community's media (or audio-visual) policy is certainly not the product of a single and unified Community vision of the sector. Instead it must be regarded as a result of a hard won compromise between both Member States and rival power centres within the institutions. The EC Treaty established the Community institutions, notably the Council of Ministers, the European Parliament (EP), the Commission and the Court of Justice of the European Communities, and it confers legislative, executive and judicial

---

32. *Why Public Service Broadcasting?* European Broadcasting Union Conference 1998. (European Broadcasting Union, 1994).
33. See European Parliament, Minutes (Provisional Edition) of the Sitting of 19 September 1996, A4–0243/96.
34. Carole Tongue is Labour MEP for London East. *The Future of Public Service Television in a Multi-channel Digital Age* can be found at <http://www.poptel.org.uk/carole-tongue/pubs/psb.html>
35. See footnote 14 on p. 11.

powers in prescribed fields upon them.[36]

Within the European Commission, the Directorate responsible for audio-visual policy is Directorate DG X (currently headed by Commissioner Marcelio Oreja) which oversees the Information, Communication, Culture and Audiovisual sectors. Its rationale includes the view that the ' . . . involvement of citizens . . . depends first of all on the capacity of European politicians and Institutions to listen to their concerns and to provide clear and rapid information'.[37] It is also responsible for providing external protection and internal support for the programme industry.

However, at least five other Directorates-General[38] also have communications-related responsibilities, though each operates from a rather different perspective from that of DG X. Thus DG I is responsible for external (economic) relations and is the representative at G7 and World Trade Organisation meetings which have recently considered the convergence of the communications sector, intellectual property rights and the liberalization of communications services. DG III, previously responsible for the internal market and now for industry, originally produced the Green Paper to be discussed below which set the scene for the major actions taken in relation to the audio-visual industry. DG IV is responsible for competition policy and plays an important role in the prevention of anti-competitive agreements and actions including monopolies and mergers, issues of great importance in relation to the recent development of the media industries. DG XIII is responsible for telecommunications, information markets and exploitation of research, again issues of considerable importance in relation to recent media developments. Finally, DG XV, responsible since 1993 for the internal market, has an interest in the liberalization of audio-visual markets. With so many different Directorates-General potentially involved, the potential for inter-institutional conflict is considerable.

The European Parliament has a Committee dealing with questions relating to information and the media; Committee XII, the Committee on Culture, Youth, Education, the Media and Sport.

---

36. EC Treaty, art 4.
37. *Welcome to DGX at the European Commission*
   <http://www.europa.eu.int/en/comm/dg10/dg10.html>
38. Many other Directorates-General are indirectly involved with media-related aspects: e.g. DGXXIV (Consumer Protection), DGXII (Science, Research and Development), etc.

This has been regarded as having low status and little influence.[39] However, as we shall see below it has had an important role in the initiation of media policy, being mainly concerned with the promotion of European integration emphasizing cultural as well as market aspects, and it has continued to play a significant role right up to and including the 1997 revision of the *Television Without Frontiers* Directive. It has also, as noted above, had a strong interest in public service broadcasting.

The European Court of Justice has heard several cases over the years, directly and indirectly involving the provision of audio-visual services or aspects thereof including some prior to the implementation of the Directive.[40] These include cases establishing the basic competence of Community action in relation to the media and those interpreting the *Television Without Frontiers* Directive and shaping its implementation. The most important cases relating to the Directive will be discussed in detail in Chapter Five below, but it may be useful at this stage to outline some of the early cases to give a flavour of the Courts' role.

The case of *Italian State v Saachi* (already discussed above) introduced the issue of the cross-border transmission of programmes – here cable retransmissions of material not authorized for broadcast under the then-prevailing Italian monopoly. The court held, distinguishing between goods and services, that the transmission of signals constituted a service and was thus subject to the Community's rules on the freedom to provide services; secondly, that the circulation of, or trade in, products used to facilitate the transmission of those signals or their materialization (e.g. on video or film) constitute goods and thus are subject to the Community's rules regarding freedom of movement of goods. However, two subsequent cases, *Coditel v Ciné Vog*[41] and *Procureur du Roi v Debauve*[42] took a position less sympathetic to the Commission as the Court upheld restrictive rules on copyright and television advertising on the grounds that the rules were not discriminatory. A different outcome was reached in *Bond Van Adverteerders v The Netherlands*[43] in which a ban on advertising was found to be discriminatory, because it was only aimed at the retransmission of

---

39. Collins, *op. cit.*, p. 31.
40. See McGonagle M., *A Textbook on Media Law*, Gill & MacMillan Ltd, 1996, Chapter 11.
41. [1980] 2 ECR. 881. Case 62/79.   42. [1980] 2 ECR 833. Case 52/79.
43. [1988] ECR 2085. Case 352/85.

foreign satellite programmes. The Court held that it could not be justified on public policy grounds.[44] Although the Court had clearly demonstrated Community competence in the area of the media, the substantive principles to be applied were by no means clear, thus opening up the need for legislative intervention. The details of that intervention and the decisions of the Court relating to it will be described in Chapter Five below.

In addition to the institutions discussed above, the Treaties create three other bodies: the Economic and Social Committee (ECOSOC), the Committee of the Regions and the European Court of Auditors. The latter examines accounts of Community institutions and is thus not directly involved in policy making. ECOSOC is an advisory board which consists of 222 members representing the interests of employers, trade unions and consumers. Its Employers' Group I[45] includes many federations, which often actively press for their interests to be taken into consideration. ECOSOC has produced opinions on its own initiative or on request from the Commission or the Council,[46] on almost every policy proposal and legislation relating to media policy. Although having a purely advisory role, its expertise has made it fairly influential.[47]

The Committee of the Regions and Local Authorities was established in 1993. The European Union Treaty gave it a common organizational structure with ECOSOC and it shares a Secretariat with that Committee. Article 198a of the Treaty specifies that the Committee is to be consulted by the Council and the Commission on issues such as new proposals for cohesion, trans-European networks, and education and training. The Committee has recently underlined the cultural importance of the audio-visual industry as safeguarding and promoting the diversity of national and regional cultures.[48] The Committee could also play an important role in

44. McGonagle, *op. cit.*, p. 275.
45. ECOSOC is divided in three groups – employers, workers and various interests (such as agriculture, small and medium sized enterprises, environment, transport, etc.).
46. The Commission, or the Council as appropriate, has to consult ECOSOC on a range of issues including agricultural matters, freedom of movement for workers, the right of establishment, social policy, internal market issues, measures of economic and social cohesion, and environmental policy. In addition, the Commission may consult it on any matter it thinks appropriate.
47. See, Kamall, S., *Spicers European Union Policy Briefings, Telecommunications Policy*, Cartermill Publishing, 1996, p. 8.
48. *Opinion on the Commission's Green Paper on strategic options to strengthen the European programme industry in the context of the audio-visual policy of the European Union.* OJEC 18 August 1995 No C210:41.

relation to the so-called 'unsolved' problem of the regions in European audio-visual policy.[49]

[49.] For a detailed overview of the issues see de Moragas Spa, M. and Garitaonandia, C., *Decentralization in the Global Era, Television in the Regions, Nationalities and Small Countries of the European Union*, John Libbey, 1995.

CHAPTER THREE

The Pan-European context

The Council of Europe

Introduction and organization

The 40-Member Council of Europe has long been concerned with audio-visual policy and regulation. For example, in 1968, the Consultative (later the Parliamentary) Assembly of the Council of Europe held a Symposium on Human Rights and Mass Communications to discuss legal problems and implications for human rights to which the printed press and increased facilities for disseminating information across frontiers gave rise.[1] Its relevance today is instructive and many of the concerns, discussions and issues dealt with during the seminar are similar to those expressed in today's debates. Media in general, and audio-visual media in particular, arc understood to be, on the one hand, aspects of general human rights (freedom of expression, balanced by the right to a private life) and, on the other, indispensable means for promoting and protecting democratic societies through the dissemination of information and the formation of public opinion. Moreover, one commentator has written that art. 10 of the Convention on Human Rights and Fundamental Freedoms, taken together with the Declaration on the Freedom of Expression and Information adopted by the Committee of Ministers on 29 April 1982, is a 'veritable European media charter.'[2] Media and communication is also a theme within the Intergovernmental Cooperation Programme.[3]

1. From the Resolution of the Assembly, Resolution 338 (1967) and see generally, *Symposium on Human Rights and Mass Communications*, Consultative Assembly, Council of Europe, 1967.
2. See Hondius F., 'Regulating Transfrontier Television – the Strasbourg Option' 1988 *Yearbook of European Law*, Vol. 8, p. 141, at p. 146.
3. *Intergovernmental Cooperation, Media and Communication* <http://www.coe. fr/eng/act-e/emedicom.htm>

The criteria currently underpinning all audio-visual and other media for the Council of Europe are that they should be 'free', 'independent' and 'pluralistic'. The three priorities for the sector are:

■ creating a genuine audio-visual area in which freedom of expression and information and the free flow of information ideas across frontiers are guaranteed;

■ developing pan-European policy measures and appropriate legal and other instruments for this purpose; and,

■ formulating appropriate measures to ensure that media law and policy keep pace with technological, economic and regulatory change in the media sector.

Currently, there are four specific concerns of the Council of Europe:[4]

■ media and democracy (including media concentrations, the implications of the new communications technologies for human rights and democracy; protection for rightsholders; and freedom of information);

■ media in a pan-European perspective, including media freedoms and training activities;

■ media and conflict, including violence in the media and protection of journalists in situations of conflict and tension;

■ media and intolerance including incitement to racial hatred.

Organizationally, the media sector has undergone important changes over the years. Media activities were dealt with by the Steering Committee on the Mass Media, or 'CDMM'. This was set up in 1976, as a unit within the Directorate of Public Law. In 1981, CDMM relocated to the Directorate of Human Rights.[5] Various specialist, expert committees meet under its general auspices. Some examples are:

■ the Group of Specialists on Media in a Pan-European Perspective (MM-S-EP) which is concerned with elaborating guidelines for the guarantee of independent public service broadcasting;

■ MM-S-NT is the Group of Specialists on the impact of new

4. *Priority Concerns* <http://www.coe.fr/eng/act-e/emedicom.htm>
5. *Directorate of Human Rights* <http://www.dhdirhr.coe.fr/Intro/eng/GENERAL/welc2dir.htm>

communications technologies on human rights and democratic values;

- The Committee of Experts on Media Concentrations and Pluralism (MM-CM) which informs itself about national developments with a view to promulgating measures to protect and promote pluralism;
- The Group of Specialists on access to official information (MM-S-AC);
- The Group of Specialists on media law and human rights (MM-S-HR)
- The Group of Specialists on the protection of rights holders in the media field (MM-S-PR), established to 'Evaluate the impact of the new communications technologies on the current level of protection for holders of copyright and neighbouring rights . . .' The Group's main interests are in the protection and management of rights in a world of multimedia, electronic and digital publishing
- Currently dealing with implications and problems caused by the use of the Internet is PC-CY, the Committee of Experts on Crime in Cyberspace. It identifies and defines crimes on the Internet and deal with issues of liability and jurisdiction.

The Parliamentary Assembly of the Council of Europe has a Sub-Committee on Media of the Committee on Culture and Education. The Assembly has adopted many Recommendations and Resolutions on audio-visual, media and journalistic matters as well as on the new communications technologies, and examples will be given below.

Binding agreements

Much of the early activity was concerned with drawing up conventions, such as:

- the European Agreement concerning programme exchanges by means of television films (1958), creating the legal framework for Eurovision;[6]
- the 1960 Agreement on the protection of television broadcasts, prohibiting unauthorized broadcasting, cable distribution, communication to the public, fixation and reproduction of

6. <http://www.coe.fr/eng/legaltxt/27e.htm>

fixations. There have also been Protocols to this Treaty in 1965, 1974, 1983 and 1989, which require parties to become parties to the 1961 Rome Convention on neighbouring rights;[7]

- the European Agreement of 1965, designed to deal with the growing phenomenon of 'pirate' broadcasts, principally from ships anchored outside territorial waters;[8] and
- the European Convention Relating to Questions on Copyright Law and Neighbouring Rights in the framework of Transfrontier Broadcasting by Satellite.[9]

The European Convention on Transfrontier Television will be dealt with more fully in a separate section in view of its importance for this study.

Non-binding recommendations

During the nineteen-eighties, several Recommendations (nonbinding instruments) were approved by the Committee of Ministers, usually on the basis of policy instruments and background reports created under the auspices of CDMM. These include the following Recommendations:

- on television advertising (R(84)3);
- on the use of satellite capacity for television and sound radio (R(84)22);
- on principles relating to copyright questions in the field of television by satellite and cable (R(86)2);
- on the production of audio-visual programmes in Europe (R(86)3), which was the basis for EURIMAGES (Resolution R(88)15). Similarly to the ECs MEDIA and AVE projects (to be discussed in the following two chapters), EURIMAGES's aim is to encourage the development of multilateral European co-productions and their distribution in Europe by way of financial support.[10]
- on sound and audio-visual copying (R(88)1);
- measures to combat piracy in the field of copyright and neighbouring rights (R(88)2);

---

7. <http://www.coe.fr/eng/legaltxt/34e.htm>
8. <http://www.coe.fr/eng/legaltxt/53e.htm>
9. <http://www.coe.fr/eng/legaltxt/153e.htm>
10. EURIMAGES <http://culture.coe.fr/Eurimages/eng/eurlist.html>

- concerning principles on the distribution of videograms having a violent, brutal or pornographic content (R(89)7).

More recent Recommendations concern:

- strategies for guaranteeing transparency in the ownership of media organisations (R(94)13;
- Recommendation of the Committee of Ministers to member States on measures against sound and audio-visual piracy (R(95)1);
- the Guarantee of the Independence of Public Service Broadcasting (R(96)10);
- the protection of journalists in situations of conflict and tension (R(96)4);
- the media and the promotion of a culture of tolerance (R(97)21);
- hate speech (R(97)20);
- the portrayal of violence in the electronic media (R(97)19);

The European Convention on Transfrontier Television

The Convention[11] aims to create a legal framework for the transfrontier circulation of television programmes, ' . . . to facilitate, among the Parties, the transfrontier transmission and the retransmission of television programme services.' (art. 1). Of course, as an international treaty, its enforceability is dependent upon the domestic arrangements of the Parties. It sets out principles concerning the rights of viewers and broadcasters and duties of states. Article 4, concerning the right to freedom of reception and transmission imposes a duty on States to; 'ensure freedom of expression and information in accordance with art 10 of the Convention . . . [to] guarantee freedom of reception and [they] shall not restrict the retransmission on their territories of programme services which comply with the terms of this Convention.' However, States, even though they should ensure that all programme services transmitted from within their jurisdiction comply with the Convention's terms (art. 5), may not interfere in the content of the programme services as this would compromise the independence of broadcasters. A right of reply for those whose honour has been impugned by a

11. European Treaty Series No. 132, 1989. See <http://www.coe.fr/eng/legaltxt/132e.htm>

transmission or whose privacy has been unwarrantably intruded upon is provided for by art. 8; art. 6(2), 'Provision of information' assists the operation of this right of reply by making it possible to identify the broadcaster.

Chapter 2 of the Treaty deals with Programming Matters. Article 7 deals with 'The Responsibilities of the Broadcaster' and provides that, in general, 'All items of programme services, as concerns their presentation and content, shall respect the dignity of the human being and the fundamental rights of others'. Programme items, in particular, shall not be 'be indecent and in particular contain pornography [or] give undue prominence to violence or be likely to incite to racial hatred.' If programmes are likely to 'impair the physical, mental or moral development of children and adolescents' then they should not be transmitted when these persons are likely to be watching them. News programmes should 'fairly present facts and events and encourage the free formation of opinions.' The issue of 'Access of the public to major events' is the subject matter of art. 9. However, it only calls on States to 'examine the legal measures to avoid the right of the public to information being undermined due to the exercise by a broadcaster of exclusive rights for the transmission or retransmission . . . of an event of high public interest and which has the effect of depriving a large part of the public in one or more other Parties of the opportunity to follow that event on television.' Thus it is more concerned with the exercise of exclusive rights than with their legitimacy as such. Article 10 symbolizes European fears that the expansion of television channels will lead inevitably to the importation and transmission of US-produced programmes. Hence the Article, entitled 'Cultural Objectives', prescribes that a majority of net transmission time (not including news, sports, teletext, advertising and game shows) should be 'where practicable' devoted to 'European works', defined in art. 2(e) as; 'creative works, the production or co-production of which is controlled by European natural or legal persons'. This is a deliberately flexible requirement, and as we shall see in Chapter Five, flexibility in the EC instruments has caused difficulties. Parties also agree to support European production (art. 10(3)) and to avoid programme services compromising the pluralism of the press or cinema (art. 10(4)). This last sub-section, derived from Recommendation R(87)7, provides that; 'No cinematographic work shall accordingly be transmitted in such services, unless otherwise agreed between its rights holders and the broadcaster, until two years have elapsed since the work was first shown in cinemas; in the case of cinematographic works co-produced by the broadcaster, this period shall be one year'.

Issues regarding advertisements and sponsorship are dealt with in the Convention in Chapter III. Various topics are covered, for example that advertisements shall be fair and honest; shall not be misleading or prejudice the interests of consumers; that advertisements 'addressed to or using children shall avoid anything likely to harm their interests and shall have regard to their special susceptibilities'; and that 'the advertiser shall not exercise any editorial influence over the content of programmes'. The percentage of time for transmitting advertisements is limited to 15 per cent of daily transmission time, which may be increased if the form of the advertisement is, for example, for direct offers of sale to the public, purchase or rental of goods or the provision of services. The form, presentation and insertion of advertisements is covered by arts 13 and 14: advertisements shall be 'clearly distinguishable as such . . . and [in principle] . . . shall be transmitted in blocks'; there shall be no subliminal or surreptitious advertisements; and they 'shall not feature, visually or orally, persons regularly presenting news and current affairs programmes'. Advertisements 'shall be inserted between programmes' or during programmes, providing a number of conditions are fulfilled. Thus in 'programmes consisting of autonomous parts, or in sports programmes and similarly structured events and performances comprising intervals, advertisements shall only be inserted between the parts or in the intervals' and the 'transmission of audio-visual works such as feature films and films made for television (excluding series, serials, light entertainment programmes and documentaries), provided their duration is more than forty-five minutes, may be interrupted once for each complete period of forty-five minutes. A further interruption is allowed if their duration is at least twenty minutes longer than two or more complete periods of forty-five minutes.' Moreover, advertisements shall 'not be inserted in any broadcast of a religious service. News and current affairs programmes, documentaries, religious programmes, and children's programmes, when they are less than thirty minutes of duration, shall not be interrupted by advertisements.' There are detailed provisions in art. 15 for particular products, namely tobacco (advertising of which is not to be permitted), alcoholic beverages and medicines and medical treatment, which have to comply with a list of rules (art. 15(2)–(4). The rules on sponsorship are contained in arts 17 and 18. No sponsorship of news and current affairs is permitted; and any sponsored programme must be clearly identified as such. The sponsor must not influence the scheduling or editorial independence of the broadcaster. No sponsor may be an entity which is the principal manufacturer or retailer of products which are prohibited from being advertised in virtue of art. 15.

The final chapter of the Convention deals with procedures in the event of violation, provisions for settlement of disputes by conciliation and arbitration, and for monitoring application. For this purpose, a Standing Committee is established by the Convention (Chapter 6). The general function of the Committee is to be 'responsible for following the application of this Convention'. Specifically, it may:

- make recommendations to the Parties concerning the application of the Convention;
- suggest any necessary modifications of the Convention and examine those proposed in accordance with the provisions of art. 23;
- examine, at the request of one or more Parties, questions concerning the interpretation of the Convention;
- use its best endeavours to secure a friendly settlement of any difficulty referred to it in accordance with the provisions of art. 25;
- make recommendations to the Committee of Ministers concerning States other than those referred to in art. 29, para 1, to be invited to accede to this Convention.

So far, the Committee (T-TT)[12] has adopted several Opinions and one Recommendation. The Opinions relate to:

- the time frame for the broadcasting of cinematographic works co-produced by the broadcaster;
- the notion of 'retransmission';
- the notion of 'broadcaster';
- certain provisions relating to advertising and sponsorship;
- freedom of reception and retransmission;

12. T-TT (97) Inf 1 (Council of Europe)

- the legal framework for 'infomercials'; and
- the application of the Convention to advertising transmitted via teletext services.

The Recommendation concerns the use of virtual images in news and current affairs programmes.

Finally, art 27 (1) deals with the relationship between the Convention and Member States of the European Community. The Article provides that, 'In their mutual relations, Parties which are members of the European Economic Community shall apply Community rules and shall not therefore apply the rules arising from this Convention except insofar as there is no Community rule governing the particular subject concerned.'

The European Convention on Human Rights

The European Convention on Human Rights has considerable relevance for the audio-visual sector, in particular because of the wording of art 10 (and to a lesser extent art 8). These are worth quoting in full.

Article 10

1. Everyone has the right to freedom of expression. This right shall include freedom to hold opinions and to receive and impart information and ideas without interference by public authority and regardless of frontiers. This article shall not prevent States from requiring the licensing of broadcasting, television or cinema enterprises.
2. The exercise of these freedoms, since it carries with it duties and responsibilities, may be subject to such formalities, conditions, restrictions or penalties as are prescribed by law and are necessary in a democratic society, in the interests of national security, territorial integrity or public safety, for the prevention of disorder or crime, for the protection of health or morals, for the protection of the reputation or rights of others, for preventing the disclosure of information received in confidence, or for maintaining the authority and impartiality of the judiciary.

Article 8

1. Everyone has the right to respect for his private and family life, his home and his correspondence.
2. There shall be no interference by a public authority with the exercise of this right except such as is in accordance with the law and is necessary in a democratic society in the interests of national security, public safety or the economic well-being of the country, for the prevention of disorder or crime, for the protection of health or morals, or for the protection of the rights and freedoms of others.

The right to freedom of expression and information recognised in art 10 includes, *inter alia*, freedom to receive and impart information and ideas by broadcasting media.[13] One commentator has noted that 'Over the years and especially since 1990, a substantial body of case law has been established by the European Court with regard to art 10 ECHR. In the legal order of the Council of Europe and its Member States, media law (whether the traditional printed press or cinematographic films), broadcasting regulations and rules on journalistic freedoms are [to be] developed and applied on this basis and within this framework'.[14] The Article applies to 'everyone', whether a natural or a legal person; it applies to original broadcasts, their retransmission or reception and it covers all forms of programming, although as Vorhoof notes, '. . . the level of protection of commercial information or advertising is to be situated on a lower level than e.g. news reporting on items of public interest or programmes in the context of public debate'.

Article 10(1) permits states to require licensing of television, broadcasting, or cinema enterprises, which has raised the question of the relationship between art 10(1) and 10(2). In *Informationsverein Lentia v Austria*,[15] the Court accepted that any authorization to license broadcasting might be 'made conditional on [technical or] other considerations including such matters as the nature and objectives of a proposed station, its potential audience at national, regional or local level, the rights and needs of a specific audience and the obligations deriving from international legal

---

13. DH-MM (7)6 para. 41 (Council of Europe, 1997)
14. Vorhoof D., 'Critical perspectives on the scope and the application of Article 10 of the European Convention on Human Rights', *Mass Media Files No 10*, Council of Europe Press, 1995.
15. 17 EHRR 93.

instruments . . . This may lead to interferences whose aims will be legitimate under the third sentence of paragraph 1, even though they do not correspond to any of the aims set out in paragraph 2.'[16] As Janis *et al.* note,[17] 'the licensing provision was held to expand the purposes for which broadcasting could be regulated through the licence procedure beyond those of paragraph 2, but the scheme would still have to satisfy the other requirements of paragraph 2, namely that the restriction be "prescribed by law" and be "necessary" in a democratic society.'

There are many cases on the legitimacy, legality and necessity of the restrictions set out in art 10(2) and which, perforce, apply to audio-visual media. Apart from the standard printed law reports, there are several other useful sources of information about such cases, such as the periodic resumés published by DH-MM, 'Case Law Concerning Article 10 of the European Convention on Human Rights.'[18] Another is *IRIS* which is the monthly bulletin of legal observations and information relevant to the European audio-visual sector (and which covers much more than reports about Council of Europe Convention cases). Finally, the Human Rights Website of the Council of Europe is also of use here. Recent judgments have considered, among other topics, journalistic coverage of racist statements protected by art 10 (*Jersild v Denmark*)[19]; seizure of film as blasphemous (*Otto-Preminger-Institut v Austria*)[20]; refusal to distribute newspaper to serving soldiers (*Vereniging Weekblad Bluf! v the Netherlands*[21]; refusal to grant a classification to a video (*Wingrove v United Kingdom*),[22]; the right of the press to criticize the courts (*De Haes and Gijsels v Belgium*[23]; freedom of critical political journalism – *Oberschlick N2 v Austria* (*Oberschlick v Austria*)[24]; restriction on the freedom of expression permitted for maintaining the authority and impartiality of the judiciary (*Worm v Austria*); broadcasting monopolies (*Telesystem Tirol Kabeltelevision v Austria*[25] and *Radio ABC v*

16. *Id.* para 32.
17. Janis M, Kay R & Bradley A, *European Human Rights Law*. Clarendon Press, Oxford, 1995.
18. DH-MM (98)6.
19. 23 September 1994, Series A vol. 298.
20. 20 September 1994, Series A vol. 295-A.
21. 9 February 1995, Series A vol. 306-A.
22. No 19/1995/525/611.   23. No. 7/1996/626/809.
24. <http://www.dhcour.coe.fr/engl//Oberschl.e.html>
25. <http://www.dhcour.coe.fr/fr/telesyst.f.html>

Austria.[26] Summaries of all these decisions are available on the Website.[27]

The Council of Europe and the information society

The Council of Europe holds periodic meetings of specialized ministers, and in that context, there have been five Ministerial Conferences on Mass Media Policy. The topic of the most recent was 'The Information Society: a Challenge for Europe'. The Conference adopted a Political Declaration and Action Plan and two resolutions, Resolution No. 1 on the impact of new communications technologies on human rights and democratic values and Resolution 2 on rethinking the regulatory framework for the media.[28]

The Action Plan concerns 'the promotion of freedom of expression and information at the pan-European level within the framework of the Information Society' and requests the Committee of Ministers of the Council of Europe, in conjunction and cooperation with other international fora, to:

- monitor the development of the Information Society and, in particular, to keep under review its effects on human rights;
- ensure regular exchanges of information and experience in this area, with a view to implementing concerted solutions at the pan-European level in the area of media law and policy;
- maintain concern regarding access to new communications and information services, in particular to work at defining a common pan-European approach as regards the content and the means for implementing universal community service;
- encourage, in particular at the transnational level, self-regulation by providers and operators of the new communications and information services, especially content providers, in the form of codes of conduct or other measures, with a view to ensuring respect for human rights and human dignity, the protection of minors and democratic values, as well as the credibility of the media themselves;
- prepare any legal instruments or other measures (binding or non-binding) which might be necessary to promote freedom of

---

26. <http://www.dhcour.coe.fr/eng/RADIO%20ABC.html>
27. <http://194.250.50.200/>
28. 5th European Ministerial Conference on Mass Media Policy. The Information Society: a challenge for Europe <http://www.dhdirhr.coe.fr/media/home.htm>

expression and information, especially across frontiers, and guarantee the protection of human rights and democratic values;

- promote transfrontier cooperation between national regulatory authorities;

- study cases of misuse of the new technologies and new communications and information services for spreading any ideology, or carrying out any activity, which is contrary to human rights, human dignity and the fundamental rights of others, as well as to the protection of minors and to democratic values, and to formulate, where necessary, any proposals for legal or other action to combat such use;

- examine the opportunity and feasibility of establishing warning, cooperation and assistance procedures, including legal ones, in liaison with other authorities, with a view to undertaking concerted action against these forms of misuse at the widest possible level;

- study the practical and legal difficulties in combating the dissemination of hate speech, violence and pornography via the new communications and information services, with a view to taking appropriate initiatives in a common pan-European framework;

- continue work in the area of media concentrations, paying particular attention to the development of new technologies and new communications and information services, with a view to undertaking any appropriate legal or policy initiatives to guarantee the maintenance of media pluralism in Europe and to study, in particular, the issue of transparency of the new communications and information services providers;

- further to study also the issue of gateway monopolies hampering access to the new technologies and new communications and information services and the accumulation of interests in both the traditional media sector and the new communications and information services sector with a view, as appropriate, to formulating proposals aimed at regulating such developments;

- study the question of exclusivity rights in the digital environment and the possible need to take further initiatives within the framework of the Council of Europe; and to

- follow closely the evolution of digital techniques and their implications for international policy concerning the protection of rights holders and the public, taking into account the work being conducted in this field in other international fora, with a view to elaborating, if necessary, legal instruments designed to supplement and coordinate the measures taken by the Member States.

Finally, The European Audiovisual Observatory[29] was set up in 1992 to enhance the transparency and availability of information on the audio-visual industry in Europe. It operates under an extended partial agreement of the Council of Europe. Apart from its specific information provision services and publications, it is arguably the most complete repository of data on all media organizations and institutions – public and private – in Europe, or relevant for Europe.

The Organization for Security and Cooperation in Europe

The Organization for Security and Cooperation in Europe (OSCE), which cooperates closely with the Council of Europe, categorizes audio-visual media matters as an aspect of the democracy and democratization of European states. The OSCE's Office of Democratic Institutions and Human Rights has conveniently compiled a thematic database, *OSCE Commitments with respect to the media*.[30] Furthermore, at the end of 1997, a new organ, the OSCE Representative on Freedom of the Media, was approved and its mandate agreed upon.[31] Based on OSCE principles and commitments, the Representative is, for an initial period of three years (renewable) to:

- observe relevant media developments;
- advocate and promote full compliance with relevant principles and commitments;
- assume an early-warning function and concentrate on a rapid response to serious non-compliance with OSCE principles and commitments;

29. <http://www.obs.coe.int/>
30. <http://www.osceprag.cz/inst/odihr/hdinfo/them/media.htm>
31. Decision No. 193 Mandate of the OSCE Representative on Freedom of the Media <http://www.osceprag.cz/news/pc-htm97/pc97-137.htm>

- address serious problems caused by obstruction of media activities and unfavourable working conditions for journalists; and
- support the Office for Democratic Institutions and Human Rights in assessing the conditions for the functioning of free, independent and pluralistic media before, during and after elections.

European Broadcasting Union

The European Broadcasting Union[32] was established in 1950 and is a non-governmental organization. Originally, it aimed to assist the solution of common legal and technical problems of European public service broadcasters. It is the world's largest professional association of national broadcasters. Following a merger with the EBU on 1 January 1993 of the International Radio and Television Organization (OIRT) (the former association of Socialist Bloc broadcasters) the expanded Union has 66 active members in 49 European and Mediterranean countries and 51 associate members in 30 countries elsewhere in Africa, the Americas, and Asia. In the course of its development, mechanisms for exchanging programmes and news have been developed. Four categories currently exist: Eurovision Network Services; Eurovision News Exchanges; Eurovision Programme Exchanges; and Euroradio. The legal sector's activities relate mainly to issues of copyright law and lawmaking, such as the acquisition of rights, lobbying on behalf of its members in European and global institutions and facilitating contractual access for non-members to the Eurovision Network. Collaboration exists between the EBU and the European Group of Television Advertising (EGTA set up in 1974) which is an association made up of 28 sales houses or commercial departments of TV channels from 22 countries which are members of the EBU. EGTA[33] concerns itself with analyzing and lobbying on all matters to do with television advertising and has recently, in conjunction with the EBU put the European Interactive Guide to TV Sponsorship on-line, thus facilitating 'all the information available on sponsorship in 40 countries and 79 channels'.[34]

32. European Broadcasting Union <http://www.ebu.ch>
33. <http://www.finaltouch.be/egtasite>
34. <http://www.finaltouch.be/egta/EGTA2_HTML/SPONSORSHIP.HTML>

European Platform of Regulatory Authorities (EPRA)

EPRA was established in April 1995, to enable regular and informal meetings of representatives of European independent regulatory authorities. As the European Institute for the Media provides the Secretariat, meetings tend to be coordinated with EIM's Television and Film Forum.[35] The meetings are used to exchange information, interpretations and applications regarding common issues of national and European media regulation.

The European Radiocommunications Office[36]

The European Radiocommunications Office (ERO) is the permanent body for European spectrum management, i.e. the allocation and assignment of spectrum frequencies. The functions of the ERO are defined in the ERO Convention and include a role in the long term planning of the radio spectrum, liaison with national frequency management authorities, coordination of research studies and consultation with interested parties on specific topics or parts of the frequency spectrum. In addition, the ERO assists the European Radiocommunications Committee (ERC) in carrying out its numerous activities. The ERC is one of three committees that form the European Conference of Postal and Telecommunications Administrations (CEPT), the regional regulatory telecommunication organization for Europe. As of 1 January 1996, 43 European countries were members of the CEPT. The ERC is concerned with the development of policy on radiocommunications issues which includes the coordination of frequencies and administrative and technical matters relating to the regulation of radio in Europe. The ERC is also responsible for preparing the European proposals and positions for conferences of the International Telecommunications Union (ITU) (the United Nations agency which regulates and coordinates global telecommunications networks and services, see http://www.itu.ch).

The ERC is supported by five permanent working groups that, within their respective areas of responsibility, prepare, and in some

35. European Institute for the Media <http://www.eim.org/epra.htm>
36. For an overview of activities <http://www.ero.dk/>

cases approve, harmonization measures in the form of European Common Proposals (ECPs) for ITU Conferences and CEPT ERC Decisions, Recommendations or Reports. To ensure that the interests of various parties involved in radiocommunications are expressed in the decision-making processes of the ERC, various consultation mechanisms have been introduced, including an annual CEPT Radio Conference and the process of Detailed Spectrum Investigations (DSI) which considers the current and future use of the frequency spectrum below 105 Ghz and has resulted in a harmonized European common frequency allocation table, to be implemented in the period up to the year 2008.

Conclusion

It is hardly surprising that the European Community is only one of a number of European organisations with an interest in broadcasting and the media generally. What is more noticeable, however, is the extent to which the broader body of norms and institutions connected with the Council of Europe provides a constitutional base for regulation at pan-European, European Union and national levels. The most striking example is of course the European Convention on Human Rights which, as noted above, has furnished a type of European media charter, and through its protections for freedom of expression and privacy performs the role undertaken by constitutional principles and court decisions in some national jurisdictions. The European Convention on Transfrontier Television and the more recent work on the information society are also of considerable importance. The activities of the European Community thus take place in an environment of international norms which further distinguish the media from purveyors of other commodities. The next chapter will describe the origins of Community media policy within this context.

CHAPTER FOUR

Origins of European community media policy

1980–84: The Parliament's concerns

A raft of reports and resolutions was presented to, and adopted by, various Committees of the European Parliament and the Parliament itself from 1980 onward. *Inter alia*, these included:

- a motion by Pedini/Hahn on a resolution on radio and television broadcasting in the European Community;[1]
- a motion on a resolution by Schinzel and others on the threat to the diversity of opinion posed by the commercialization of the new media;[2]
- a resolution of the European Parliament of 16 January 1981 on the information policy of the European Community, of the Commission of the European Communities and of the European Parliament, which was critical of the Community's information policy – or, rather, lack of one.[3] This lack meant that, '23 years after the signature of the EEC Treaty, the level of information about the Community among the citizens of the Member States remains low . . . ';
- the Hahn Report and Resolution on radio and television broadcasting in the European Community.[4] The report includes the Opinion of the Legal Affairs Committee to the effect that there should be a policy of approximating broadcasting laws within Member States.

The latter Resolution is of some importance given the development of future policy and is worth summarizing. After noting earlier action concerned with, *inter alia*, the alleged threat to diversity

1. Doc. 1-409/80.   2. Doc. 1-422/80.
3. OJ No C 28, 9-2-81, based on the Schall report (Doc. 1-596/80).
4. OJ No C 1982 of 5 April 1982, p. 110.

of opinion posed by commercialization of the new media, the Resolution stressed the need for all citizens of the Member States to receive authentic information on Community policy and thus to be given a share in political responsibility. Radio and television had become the chief media for informing and shaping public opinion, but reporting of European Community problems in the past had been inadequate and in many cases negative, whilst citizens of Europe had a serious lack of information on Community issues. The introduction of transmission by satellite and the development of cable systems would vastly increase broadcasting capacity via the additional channels and make it possible to reach all regions of Europe simultaneously. The Resolution expressed concern that if the European Community and its institutions did not participate in the decision-making process about the new forms of media delivery, developments might take place which would not be in the interest of the Community. Moreover, the role and involvement of publicly controlled broadcasting corporations in the Member States was considered to be of paramount importance in ensuring the development of appropriate policies and initiatives in the interests of the people of the Community. The Resolution thus called on the Commission to submit a report on the media and to create the political and legal basis for the realization of a European television channel providing a full range of programmes, covering news, politics, education, culture, entertainment and sport; it should be European in origin, transmission range, target audience and subject matter. More importantly, as it turned out, the Resolution also proposed that outline rules should be drawn up on European radio and television broadcasting, with a view *inter alia* to protecting young people and establishing a code of practice for advertising at European level.

Underlying this Resolution was thus a belief in the value and desirability of European unification and that information sharing on a European level was the key which would act as the counterweight to national (or at best, regional) reporting. This perception of broadcasting underscored the notion put forward by, among others, President Mitterrand of France, that Europe has a 'cultural dimension' and that broadcasting should be seen neither primarily as a cultural good nor an economic commodity but as an instrument of forging a European identity. This view was endorsed in an interim Report by the Commission.[5] The Report surveyed Member

5. Interim Report – *Realities and Tendencies in European Television: Perspectives and Options*. Doc COM (83)229 (final) of 25 May 1983.

State's broadcasting laws. It also put forward a proposal to create a European broadcasting channel, which would help to create, foster and cement European consciousness and identity. This became the rather short-lived EUROPA-TV. Neverthless, despite the prominence of the theme of integration through the provision of information by means of a European channel, the basis was laid for the gradual process of moving towards European rules relating to retransmission, programming and advertising, which as we shall see in Chapter Five is the first theme for action taken up by the *Television Without Frontiers* Directive.

In 1984, the Parliament adopted a Resolution[6] on the basis of the Arfe Report 'on a policy commensurate with new trends in European television' proposing the setting up of a European Community Fund for Programme Production, fixing the level of aid in proportion to the programmes broadcast in the Member States. This was to form the second plank of the strategy discussed in Chapter Five below. The Resolution also called for the development of a European legal framework for broadcasting. Yet another Resolution and Report were adopted, 'on broadcast communication in the European Community', echoing earlier concerns, and focused on the threat to diversity of opinion by the over-commercialization of the media and its ownership in a few hands.[7] In sum, the Parliament had by 1984 expressed a wide variety of different concerns relating to the European media and demanded action on the key issues which were to become central to later Community media policy. What was however clearly lacking was a coherent approach; the Resolutions seemed to offer a rag-bag of individual policies with little overall coherence, partly reflecting the varied rationales for action discussed earlier.

Also in 1984, the Ministers responsible for cultural affairs met for the first time in the Council of Ministers. They resolved:

- to set up a production fund for film and tv;
- to draw up common measures to ensure that television programmes had a minimum European content;
- to set up a sequence for film distribution – cinema exhibition, television screening then video sales.

Most significantly for Community legislation, 1984 saw the

6. OJ No C 117 30 April 1984 based on Report Doc. 1-1541/83.
7. OJ No C 127 based on Report Doc. 1-1523/83 (the Hutton Report).

publication of the Green Paper 'on the establishment of the common market for broadcasting, especially by satellite and cable', and this will now be discussed in detail.[8]

As we have seen, the concerns of the Parliament were largely based on the provision of information and on the need for cultural integration. By the mid-eighties, however, audio-visual policy was also firmly within the Single Internal Market framework. What mattered now was the creation of 'legal conditions necessary for the establishment of internal markets with a European dimension . . .'[9] The essence of policy was to transform national broadcasting markets into an integrated European-wide market for broadcast services, and the first major statement of this can be found in the 1984 Green Paper.

The Green Paper

This Green Paper on the establishment of the common market for broadcasting, especially by satellite and cable, reflects a number of themes and issues which have been identified by Schwartz, who was intimately involved in Commission decision-making,[10] as critical for the Community's approach to an unrestricted broadcast environment. The Paper was lengthy and complex; the practical results will be described in the following chapter. However, here it is necessary to summarize the main concerns in the Green Paper, and selected information will be given on the legal context in which they operated.

Freedom of transmission

The Commission's fundamental objective was to create a legal framework to remove impediments to the flow of television transmissions. The legal basis for the proposals involved two different sets of provisions. First there was Article 10(1) of the Council of Europe European Convention on Human Rights setting out the right to freedom of expression and secondly, Articles 59 and 62 of the Treaty of Rome on freedom to provide services within the Community. Thus unrestricted transmissions were regarded as a specific manifestation of the fundamental right laid down in

8. COM(84)300 final.   9. Schwartz, *op.cit.* p. 36.   10. *ibid.*

Article 10(1) through forming a means of freedom of expression across national frontiers regardless of media employed. Secondly, as we have seen, television programmes had been defined by the European Court of Justice in *Saachi,* as 'services' by virtue of their nature and as services provided for remuneration (article 60). Accordingly, freedom of services had to be provided in the audiovisual sector. Three implications followed from this:[11]

- nationals in one Member State should be able to supply services to nationals resident in another Member State without having any restriction put on the distribution of that service by the government of the receiving Member State (see arts 59 and 62 of the Treaty);
- if a programme was legally broadcast in one Member State, then there could be no supervisory arrangements in another Member State to protect that country's national broadcasting arrangements. In other words, broadcasters in one Member State have the right to have their programmes transmitted in another Member State's territory without interference from the authorities in that State. Put differently, listeners and viewers in one Member State can exercise their right to receive programmes free from any discrimination or restriction whether the programmes are received directly or by cable and beamed via land-based transmitters or via satellite;
- authorized cable companies should be able to practice their right to receive transmissions from other Member States without interference from their own national authorities and to relay them simultaneously and unchanged.

A second theme in the Paper relevent to freedom of transmission was that of prohibition of discrimination against foreign broadcasts.[12] Thus any measure which imposes on transmissions from another Member State (whether relayed by satellite or by cable) conditions which are more stringent than those imposed on domestic broadcasters was to be prohibited and, if it existed, was to be removed.

A further important issue was that of non-discriminatory restrictions on foreign broadcasters, which 'take the form of provisions that become applicable to both domestic and foreign

---

11. See the Green Paper, *op. cit.,* Part Five.
12. See the Green Paper, *op. cit.,* Part Five B.

transmissions once the latter are being received and transmitted in the country in question'.[13] The Treaty restricts indiscriminately applicable provisions if the restriction affects the freedom to provide services. Possible examples were:

(a) copyright claims;
(b) extension of the scope of advertising restrictions to foreign transmissions relayed by domestic cable systems; and
(c) imposing on foreign broadcasts national requirements applicable to other programmes.

The principle sought to be achieved by the Commission here was that of the freedom to provide services which follows from the admissibility and desirability of cross-frontier transmission of broadcast programmes as a matter only for the law of the transmitting country. There were, however, two exceptions to this principle:

■ where restriction in the recipient country is justified on grounds of 'general interest'; see the *Debauve* case below;[14]
■ applicability of rules justified on grounds of literary and artistic copyright; see the *Coditel* case below.[15]

Justifications for discrimination or exemptions from the prohibition against discrimination were also considered in some depth in the Green Paper. Under art. 56(1) there are three grounds which justify exemptions from the prohibition of discrimination on foreign programming: public policy; public security; or public health; and it is unlikely that these would justify the application of different restrictions to domestic broadcasting and that from other Member States.[16] In accordance with art. 56(1), in the *Rutili* case[17] the ECJ endorsed the principles of freedom of nationals to transmit, freedom of reception, and freedom of distribution unless there is a 'sufficiently serious threat to the fundamental interests of society recognized as such by the Community'.[18] Any special rules restricting foreign broadcasts must also be specially justified as a specific manifestation of the general principle of art. 10 of the Eu-

---

13. Schwartz, *op. cit.*, p. 40.
14. *Procureur du Roi v Debauve* [1980] 2 ECR 833. Case 52/79.
15. *Coditel v Cine Vog* [1980] 2 ECR 881. Case 62/79.
16. See Schwartz, *op. cit.*
17. *Rutili v Minister for the Interior* [1975] ECR 1219. Case 36/75.
18. Schwartz, *op. cit.*, p. 26.

ropean Convention on Human Rights and so as generally necessary in a democratic society.

Programme content

Apart from issues concerning freedom of transmission, the Green Paper also had implications for programme content through considering the issue of restriction on cross-border transmissions due to differences in laws in Member States which aim to protect the public interest or public order.[19] Indeed, the Parliament, in the 1982 Resolution referred to above, had already anticipated this and resolved that 'outline rules should be drawn up on European radio and television broadcasting, inter alia, with a view to protecting young people and establishing a code of practice for advertising at European level'. The Commission also proposed that 'a law protecting minors in relation to broadcasting with a European-wide minimum standard could provide to be a necessary corollary to liberalising the provision of broadcasting services between Community countries'.[20] The House of Lords Select Committee's Report on the Green Paper noted that 'Those witnesses who touched on the point supported a Community Code of Practice'.[21]

Right of reply

Another topic relating to general programming contained in the Green Paper was that of the right to reply.[22] The Commission surveyed national arrangements and concluded that, while it might be desirable to have a uniform system of rules for all Member States, especially on the question of whether a person resident in one country could avail himself of the right in another country, mere desirability could not avoid the conclusion that there was little evidence to show that existing arrangements constituted an impediment to international broadcasting. The Commission therefore doubted whether Community action was required, proposed further discussion and the Green Paper made proposals for a possible Directive if this were to be required.

---

[19]. Green Paper, *op. cit.*, Parts Five C VI, Six B.
[20]. Green Paper, *op. cit.*, p. 288.   [21]. HL 43 (1985–86), para. 83.
[22]. Green Paper, *op. cit.*, Part Six B III.

Advertising

The Green Paper proposed harmonizing rules concerning advertising within Member States.[23] The Court of Justice in the case of *Procureur du Roi v Debauve*[24] had, as in *Saachi*,[25] reaffirmed that the broadcasting of television signals including cable retransmission came within the Treaty of Rome's provisions on the freedom to provide services. However, this only required the lifting of restrictions where discrimination was based on nationality. The Belgian law did not discriminate between foreign or national broadcasters and in the absence of any European rules on the matter each Member State could decide, on public interest grounds, whether or not to permit advertising. The Commission took the view that it was thus necessary to propose harmonization of the European rules governing broadcast advertising including restriction on the total amount of advertising time as a proportion of broadcast time, permitting the retransmission of advertisements from other Member States on Sundays, public holidays and at times other than when it was permitted for national broadcasters to advertise, drawing up rules affecting tobacco and alcohol advertisements and rules regarding the distinction between programmes and advertisements and sponsorship.

Copyright

Finally, in relation to copyright, the *Coditel 1*[26] decision meant that, as with advertising rules, national copyright law, non-discriminately applied, may be a ground for restricting the freedom of circulation of programmes within the Community. Copyright holders could claim that the reception of copyright material in territories for which no licence had been granted was not permitted, but in any case, satellite broadcasting footprints meant that it was inevitable that some reception might fall out with the copyright area. For example, BBC and IBA programmes were being received in Ireland and Belgium with no benefit accruing to the rights holders, although in the latter case the BBC had concluded a contract covering the retransmission by cable of BBC programmes worth £1.5 million. *Coditel* concerned the retransmission by a Belgian

23. Green Paper, *op. cit.*, Parts Five C IV, Six A.
24. [1980] 2 ECR 833 Case 52/79.   25. *Italian State v Saachi* [1974] 1 ECR 409.
26. [1980] 2 ECR 881 Case 62/79.

concern, Coditel, of a German broadcast, which included the film *Le Boucher*. The exclusive distribution rights in Belgium had been granted to Cine Vog, which brought an action for breach of copyright against Coditel and the film's owners. Coditel argued that any restriction would conflict with the Treaty's provisions on freedom to provide services. The Court ruled that the grant of exclusive rights limited to a national territory did not affect the common market in broadcasting contrary to the Treaty. After negotiations, Belgian cable companies concluded a contract with twelve channels in five countries to facilitate the buying of licences to enable copyright material to be used.

The Commission, in the Green Paper, considered several approaches, as the *Coditel* judgment was, in its view, not favourable to the creation of a common market in broadcasting. It considered treating broadcasts as if they were material works but concluded that this was not appropriate; the use of contractual arrangements, but this would be impractical because of the numbers of parties potentially involved; and the creation of a Community-wide licensing agency, but this would again be impractical. The Commission did not consider a further option of transferring copyright on retransmission to the original (but not retransmitting) broadcasters and it advocated instead the introduction of a statutory licence, granted for remuneration, as a means of achieving liberalization. The effect would be that any entity retransmitting works would be permitted to do so, but that rights holders would have a statutory right to 'equitable remuneration' determined either according to various principles or by arbitration, if necessary.

The House of Lords Select Committee noted that the Commission's copyright proposals were criticized by almost every witness, for example, because copyright is not a restriction on the flow of broadcasts; because statutory licencing is against the law of most Member States; because voluntary contracts do work well; and because rights holders should be able to negotiate their own fee and/or stop their material from being used. Indeed, it was alleged that the quantity of material might actually drop if rights holders were reluctant to sell the rights initially, and it was argued that the compulsory licensing scheme was outside the Community's powers as it would prejudice Member States' rules governing intellectual property, contrary to art. 222 of the Treaty. The Committee concluded that the Green Paper had not made out a case for Community regulation along the lines proposed; that the proposal for the statutory licencing system was not the best approach; and, that rights holders should not be deprived of either their freedom to negotiate fees or to restrain their material from being used. The evolution of negotiated agreements was the way forward.[27]

This discussion of the Green Paper and its background sets the scene for our detailed examination of the Directive *Television Without Frontiers* in the next chapter; it was here that these issues were finally resolved. However, it should also be noted briefly that these regulatory concerns of the Commission were not the only field of action with relevance to the media; there were two others which also bore some degree of fruit later.

Support systems for the audio-visual industry

MEDIA

The main measure to promote the development of the European audio-visual industry rejoices in the acronym MEDIA, the programme which aims to create 'Measures to Encourage the Development of the Industry of Audio-visual Production [later of the European Audiovisual Industry]. It was 'addressed to audio-visual professionals'[28] and the first phase was established within the Community's own resources in the context of the Media '92 pilot programme. It lasted from 1987–91, after several reports from both the Parliament and the Commission proposing audio-visual production support measures.[29] Areas chosen for support were production, distribution, training, and financing. The initial budget was ECU 1 million which grew to ECU 7.5 million by 1989. Maggiore describes MEDIA 92 thus: 'MEDIA 92 acts from a global European point of view, and this is its principal virtue. It is the living proof that the European institutions are the only convenient seat for the development of a genuine and effective European audiovisual policy.'[30]

The Council of Ministers adopted the programme officially on

27. HL 67, *op. cit.*
28. See MEDIA CECA-CEE-CEEA Bruxelles, Luxembourg 1991 p. 3.
29. See Collins R, *op.cit.*, Ch 6.
30. Maggiore, M, *op. cit.*, p. 65.

December 20 1991,[31] allocating a budget of approx. ECU 200 million for the 1991–95 period, after the pilot phase had been evaluated by a Committee of Experts. MEDIA was organized on the basis of geographically dispersed management of the various actions and programmes with overall coordination by the EC. It had five policy principles:

- creating a Single European Market for audio-visual services and thus taking advantage of the effect of the scale of the single market for the film and tv programme industry;
- developing cross-border networks of professionals which aim to diminish the fragmentation and dispersion of talent within the audio-visual sector; the professionals themselves would define the criteria, procedures and management of these initiatives;
- placing special focus on SMEs with particular incentive schemes for enterprises in countries with 'less widespread' cultures and languages;
- injection of seed capital which cannot exceed 50 per cent of the total capital required and aiming to produce self-sufficient and self-financing projects; and
- creation of a 'coherent set of complementary and interactive actions covering all the industrial functions upstream and downstream of production' thus permitting an initiative to be cumulatively supported by various programmes.

The Commission put forward a Communication evaluating MEDIA which was generally positive. It proposed further improvements towards;

- increasing the competitive capacity of audio-visual products;
- extending the structural action by the crossborder regrouping of businesses;
- increasing the effort for financial mobilization; and
- strengthening management control by setting up a computerized follow-up tool.

This was followed by a Communication recommending an action programme to promote the development of MEDIA and a proposal for a Council Decision to strengthen its budgetary and

---

31. *Decision Concerning the Implementation of an Action Programme to Promote the Development of the European Audiovisual Industry (MEDIA) (1991–1995).* OJ L 380. 31/12/90 pp. 37–44; the Expert report is MEDIA (1990): *Progress report of the Pilot Projects. September 1990. MEDIA 92.* CEC Brussels.

organizational aspects. Further detailed discussion will follow in Chapter Four below.

The Community has also become involved in another support mechanism called Audio-visual Eureka, which emerged out of the First *Assises de l'audiovisuel* held in 1989 and organized by the Committee of Coordinators of the audio-visual EUREKA. It is an intergovernmental, pan-European programme aiming at the 'the emergence of a truly European market and area of cooperation within the audio-visual sector' and was established under Common Declaration on 2 October 1989. The European Community is an associate member.[32] This will also be discussed more fully in Chapter Six.

Technological programmes[33]

During the mid-nineteen-eighties, several technical programmes were adopted by the Community. Two main areas were targetted for action: a common standard for satellite television transmissions and the development of high-definition television. The basic rationale for the development of such programmes was the drive towards unified standards permitting the maximum convergence of technologies and, thus, circulation of programming via compatible transmission and reception media.

On 3 November 1986, the Council of Ministers adopted a Directive 'on the adoption of common technical specifications of the MAC/packet family of standards for direct satellite television broadcasting.'[34] This measure was adopted to implement 'common technical specifications' in order to simplify 'the broadcasting of television programmes in all countries of the Community' and to make 'a significant contribution to European unification and to the development of a true European identity'. This would, furthermore, lead to 'the creation of a large unified market, on which products will be freely exchanged without any technical barriers,

---

32. Welcome to Audio-visual EUREKA <http://www.aveureka.be> A third mechanism exists as a partial agreement within the Council of Europe: EURIMAGES, or European Support Fund for the Co-production and Distribution of Creative Cinematographic; this was established by decision No. 15 of the Committee of Ministers and started its operation on 1 January 1989 <http://www.coe.fr/eng/act%2De/eapeurim.htm>

33. See Collins R., *op. cit.*, Chapter 7, 'The Technological Conundrum' and Maggiore M., *op. cit.*, Chapter 4, 'The Technological Challenge'.

34. 86/529/EEC; OJ 1986 L311/28.

which will be of great economic benefit for the European consumer electronics industry as regards its competitiveness'. The
Directive was only valid until 1991. It was replaced by the 1992
Directive on the adoption of standards for satellite broadcasting of
television signals.[35] Collins expresses the view that ' . . . the Directives on television transmission standards . . . express the dominant
assumptions in the Community of the early and mid 1980s; that a
single broadcast market would unify the Community culturally
(and therefore politically) and would assist the development of the
Community's audio-visual hardware and software industries.
However, neither Directive established the single market which
they were conceived to implement.'[36]

Secondly, from an earlier stage action was taken to promote
High Definition Television (HDTV).[37] This project was the first
major EUREKA initiative in the audio-visual area and was called
EUREKA 95 – HDTV. It began in 1986 as an R&D development
involving four major European electronics companies: Bosch in
Germany, Philips in the Netherlands, Thomson in France and
Thorn-EMI in the United Kingdom.[38] The objective was to improve the picture quality through evolving from 625 lines to 1,250
lines and incorporating CD quality sound reproduction. It also involved changing the screen format, from the existing 4:3 aspect
ratio to 16:9 wide-screen format, thus eliminating the need for
'vertical contraction' whenever cinema films were broadcast on
television. The HDTV programme was formalized in a 1989 Decision but represented a major policy failure.[39] Once more, the
somewhat unsatisfactory later history of standardization and
HDTV will be examined in Chapter Six.

Conclusion

It is unsurprising after the material covered in the earlier chapters
of this book that the origins of Community media law and policy
do not present a coherent picture. Thus we first have action by the
Parliament with a strong emphasis on cultural integration and the
provision of information by the Community, with important deci-

---

[35.] 92/38/EEC.   [36.] *op.cit.* 114.   [37.] 89/337/EEC: OJ 1989 L 142/1.
[38.] High Definition: EUREKA 95s Pioneering Role <http://www.eureka.be/home/
ek-news/av-dos.htm#High_def>
[39.] 89/337/EEC.

sions of the Court of Justice emphasising the nature of broadcasting as the provision of a service. The Green Paper of 1984 was a lengthy and complex document and, as the reactions of the House of Lord's Select Committee showed, its proposals were not entirely uncontroversial. Nor did the early attempts to provide support and technical programmes for the media industries represent a wholly coherent approach to the issues involved.

Nevertheless, the basic building blocks for developing policy were already in place by the late 1980s. In the next two chapters we shall describe how they were turned into action through legislation and further development of support programmes.

CHAPTER FIVE

The *Television Without Frontiers* Directive

The development of audio-visual policy by the European Union is determined by a twofold objective: to establish and ensure the functioning of a genuine European space for audio-visual services and to contribute to developing a strong, forward-looking programme industry that can compete on world markets and help European culture to flourish and create jobs in Europe.[1] These two objectives, linked to the development of the market and to industrial policy, are being pursued by taking account of the cultural dimension of the audio-visual sector, and can be seen both in terms of the regulatory framework governing the European audio-visual area and in various support initiatives.[2] As suggested above, the Community's overall approach thus alternates between treating the sector as a cultural good or treating it as an economic commodity.

The *Television Without Frontiers* Directive

On 3 October 1989 the Council adopted Directive 89/552/EEC, *On the co-ordination of certain provisions laid down by law, regulation or administrative action in Member States concerning the pursuit of television broadcasting activities,* commonly known as the *Television Without Frontiers* Directive (the Directive).[3]

[1.] See 'European Trump Cards In A Game With Global Players: EU Audio-visual Policy', speech by Mr Oreja, Member of the Commission, Medientage, Munchen – 14.10.1997. In addition to these objectives, the Commission monitors closely the emergence and development of new audio-visual and information services, with emphasis on their impact on creation, communication and fundamental rights.

[2.] *First Report On The Consideration Of Cultural Aspects In European Community Action,* (European Commission, 1994), Part III 'Audio-visual Policy'.

[3.] OJ 1989 L 298/23.

Member States were required to incorporate the rules laid down in the Directive into their own laws on television broadcasting by 3 October 1991. The Directive is the cornerstone of the regulatory framework for the European Union in respect of audio-visual services. Its principal objective is to permit the free circulation of television broadcasts in the European Union and thereby to encourage the development of transnational services. It is consequently based on arts 57(2) and 66 of the EC Treaty. The Community felt that a Directive was needed following the judgment of the Court of Justice of the European Communities in the *Debauve* case in 1980;[4] the Court there accepted that pending harmonization of the law at Community level a Member State was entitled to prevent the retransmission of television advertisements from other Member States on grounds of public interest.

The method used in the Directive is that of the coordination of national rules where that is necessary, so that the disparities between them can no longer constitute legal obstacles to the free circulation of televised broadcasts. Free circulation is the principal objective of the directive, but it also takes into account other objectives such as the protection of consumers and minors, the promotion of the European audio-visual industries, the protection of public health, etc. Free circulation is based on a double principle of unity of the applicable law and of freedom to receive broadcasts (art. 2):

- each broadcaster may be subject to the laws of only the single Member State under whose jurisdiction it falls (or is established) and must comply with a minimum of common rules in so-called 'coordinated' fields;
- Member States must not impede the reception or retransmission on their territory of broadcasts originating from other Member States for reasons falling within the coordinated fields.

The coordinated fields include the definition of criteria whereby a broadcaster is deemed to fall within the jurisdiction of a Member State, televisual and sponsored advertising (amount of advertising and message content), the protection of minors, the right of reply and a specific provision devoted to the promotion of the production and distribution of audio-visual programmes through quotas.

Interestingly (but reflecting our comments in earlier chapters),

---

4. *Procureur du Roi v Debauve* [1980] 2 ECR 833 Case 52/79.

in the recitals to the Directive, there is also an acknowledgement that there is a much broader principle at stake than merely freedom to provide goods and services,[5] namely, freedom of expression as enshrined in art. 10(1) of the European Convention of Human Rights of the Council of Europe, ratified by all EU Member States. Freedom of broadcasting under the Directive must, therefore, be in accordance with art. 10(1). The CJEC has for instance examined exclusive rights to broadcasting in light of that principle.[6]

Revision of the Directive

Article 26 of the 1989 Directive provided that, no later than the end of the fifth year after the date of adoption of the Directive and every two years thereafter, the Commission must submit to the European Parliament, the Council and the Economic and Social Committee a report on the application of the Directive and, if necessary, make further proposals to adapt it to developments in the field of television broadcasting. The first report on the application of the Directive[7] concluded that it was necessary to revise it, in order to adapt it to developments in the European audio-visual field. The proposal for amendment put forward in May 1995 by the Commission was the subject of detailed discussions within the Community institutions over more than two years. The review took place against the background of the Commission's Green Paper and the case law produced by the CJEC relating to the clarification of the Directive. The Commission's Green Paper on audio-visual policy of April 1994[8] was offered in the context of the Commission's White Paper on Growth, Competitiveness and Employment, especially the proposals for a European information infrastructure. Concentrating on the development of the European film and television programme industry, the Green Paper argues that a coordinated European approach to restructuring the industry is needed if it is not to decline further in the coming years. The Green Paper also appears to view this market growth generated by

5. See, McGonagle, M., *op. cit*, pp. 274–281.
6. *Elliniki Radiophonia Tiléorass-Anonimi Etairia v Dimotiki Etairia Pliroforissis*, Case No C-260/89, 18 June 1991, [1991] ECRI-2925.
7. COM(95)86 final, 31 May 1995.
8. European Commission, *Strategy Options to Strengthen the European Programme Industry in the Context of the Audio-visual Policy of the European Union*, COM(94)96 final.

new technology (digital systems) and liberalization as a threat to, rather than an opportunity for, the European industry. The co-decision procedure[9] led to the adoption of European Parliament and Council Directive 97/36/EC amending Directive 89/552/EEC on 30 June 1997. The new Directive came into force on the day of its publication in the Official Journal of the European Communities on 30 July 1997.[10] Directive 97/36/EC amends art. 26 of Directive 89/552/EEC to provide that the next report on the application of the Directive should be submitted no later than the end of the third year after the date of adoption of the Directive (i.e. 31 December 2000). The other amendments mainly set out to complete and clarify various definitions, notably as regards Member States' jurisdiction over broadcasters, to introduce rules governing teleshopping and to increase protection for children. On second reading, the European Parliament tabled amendments relating particularly to the protection of children, the introduction of the 'v-chip' and, above all, the broadcasting of sporting events. A more detailed analysis follows.

Coverage of the Directive

The 1989 Directive, and its review, are the result of considerable pulling and pushing between various interest groups and governments and must be understood in this context.[11] It is composed of twenty-six Articles divided into seven Chapters,[12] and almost every Article has been a topic of debate. Copyright was omitted (the 'missing chapter')[13] as no agreement about it could be reached.

---

9. Media matters have been, since Maastricht, legislated according to the co-decision procedure. This procedure, described in art. 189(b) of the European Union Treaty, came into force after the ratification of the Treaty at the end of 1993. It was devised to enhance democratic control in EC decision-making, which was virtually non-existent at the time, by giving the EP real co-legislative powers. This means that instead of simply being consulted on draft decisions, regulations or directives, it can effectively negotiate and at the end can even decide to reject a proposal entirely. It also means the EP can have a stronger impact on EC audio-visual policies.
10. OJ 1997 L 202/60.
11. For a detailed overview of how the Directive was established see Collins R., *op. cit.* pp. 53–80; Humphreys P.J., *op. cit.* pp. 264–79; Hirsch M. and Petersen V.G., 'Regulation of Media at the European Level' in Siune K. and Truetzschler W., *Dynamics of Media Politics. Broadcast and Electronic Media in Western Europe*, Sage, 1992, pp. 42–56.
12. For a detailed description see, Wallace R. and Goldberg D., 'The EEC Directive on Television Broadcasting', *op. cit.*
13. Collins R., *op. cit*, p. 73.

The main problem to be addressed by the Directive, and the reason why, finally, most Member States were favourably disposed towards it, was that satellite broadcasting, in conjunction with cable delivery systems, had the capacity to spill over national boundaries, with the result that Member States were not in a position to regulate them.

The Directive begins by defining television broadcasting, broadcaster, television advertising, surreptitious advertising, sponsorship and teleshopping. Article 1 defines 'television broadcasting' as the initial transmission by cable or over the air, including that by satellite, in unencoded or encoded form, of television programmes intended for reception by the public (i.e. point-to-multipoint). It includes the communication of programmes between undertakings with a view to their being relayed to the public. The 1997 Directive took account of changes in the market, particularly those arising from technological developments but without extending the scope of the Directive to the new on-line audio-visual services such as video-on-demand (as originally proposed in the Green Paper on Audio-visual Policy). Furthermore, a definition of what constitutes a broadcaster has now been introduced.[14]

Article 2(1) provides the criterion for determining which country should have jurisdiction over a broadcaster and art. 2(2) lays down the principle of the basic freedom of transmission. The application of the 1989 Directive revealed, however, the need to clarify the concept of jurisdiction as applied specifically to the audio-visual sector; when Member States came to implement the directive at national level, differing interpretations of the provisions on jurisdiction became evident. The UK for instance chose to use satellite uplink as the basis of jurisdiction.[15] That was the criterion used in the Council of Europe's Convention on Transfrontier Television, which predated the Directive and was to some extent a model for European broadcasting regulation. However, other Member States used the broadcaster's place of establishment. Case law of the Court of Justice of the European Communities (see below), made clear that the establishment criterion should be used

---

14. Broadcaster means the natural or legal person who has editorial responsibility for the composition of schedules of television programmes and who transmits them or has them transmitted by third parties.

15. Uplink is the technical process whereby programmes are broadcast from a specific transmitter on earth to a satellite, from where they are subsequently downlinked back to satellite receivers on earth.

as the principal criterion determining the jurisdiction of a particular Member State. The revised Directive states therefore clearly that establishment shall be the basis of jurisdiction, and sets out a hierarchy of criteria for defining the place of establishment of broadcasters. A broadcaster's place of establishment is generally held to be the place in which it has its head office and where decisions about programming content are made. It is also confirmed in the revised Directive that, as a general rule, the Member States must ensure freedom of reception and must not restrict the retransmission on their territories of television broadcasts from other Member States for reasons falling within the fields coordinated by the Directive.

Member States however, remain free to require television broadcasters under their jurisdiction to comply with more detailed or stricter rules in the areas covered by this Directive, according to art. 3. The most important innovation included in the 1997 Directive concerns the broadcasting of major events (particularly sport), which is contained in a new art. 3a. The Member States may each draw up a list of events which must be broadcast unencrypted even if exclusive rights have been bought by pay-television stations. On the basis of the principle of mutual recognition, they must ensure that the various broadcasters respect each of these lists. The events concerned may be of national or of other significance, such as the Olympic Games, the World Cup or the European Football Championship. These provisions apply to contracts concluded after the publication of the Directive and relate to events taking place after its entry into force.

Articles 4–6, which are highly controversial, are concerned with quotas. Member States must ensure that broadcasters reserve the majority of transmission time (art 4) for European works, the fear being that American programmes will otherwise swamp the European market. The types of programmes excluded from the quotas (news, sports, events, games, advertising and teletext services) indicate that the concern is for the European film industry and for drama production. The duty is however watered down by the use of phrases such as 'where practicable and by appropriate means' and 'to be achieved progressively'. Article 5 deals with quotas for independent works (10 per cent), the aim being to safeguard the smaller independent sector. The definition of 'European works' and the definition of the origin of the works by reference to the residence of authors and workers appear in art. 6. 'Authors' appears to include the director and writers of the screen play and music, and 'workers' would include actors and film crew. The imprecise language of the Directive accords Member States huge discretion in tailoring the quota to fit their own needs. For example, France enacted a more stringent standard (60 per cent minimum of European works and 40 per cent minimum of Francophone productions)[16] with heavy penalties for non-compliance. In this respect, the Directive is clearly protectionist. The US challenged the Directive under the General Agreement on Tariffs and Trade (GATT) immediately after the Directive was formally adopted. The two principal purposes of the GATT are to reduce tariffs and other barriers to trade, and to eliminate discrimination in the treatment accorded to imports from different countries. The US claimed that, as a trade restriction, the quota contravened the GATT and that the US entertainment industry's products should be subject to free trade rules, thus guaranteeing access to foreign markets. In response, the Europeans, galvanized by the French position, lobbied hard for an affirmative cultural exception to the GATT.[17] The end result was that negotiators were unable to reach an acceptable compromise and the Directive was able to stand, as ultimately the US proved unwilling to sacrifice the entire Uruguay round for the sake of its entertainment industry. The current position has by no means resolved the question of cultural imperialism, and the affirmative cultural exception in the GATT[18] for the audio-visual service sector (which includes movies, television, home video and musical recordings) is due to be reconsidered soon.

A review of the impact of the quotas revealed that:

> The European works quota has had no impact on the major broadcasters in each Member State, particularly as the public service networks already transmitted the necessary level of programming in response to market demand and their public service remit. While the quota might have been expected to have an impact on newly established or thematic channels which do not

---

16. Member States could not impose quotas for domestically-produced works, but they could do so on the basis of language criteria.

17. See Wilkins K.L., 'Television Without Frontiers: An EEC Broadcasting Premiere' in *Boston College International and Comparative Law Review*, Volume XIV, Winter 1991, No. 1, pp. 195–211.

18. General Agreement on Tariffs and Trade: Multilateral Trade Negotiations Final Act Embodying the Results of the Uruguay Round of Trade Negotiations, art xxix(2)(b), Apr 15, 1994, 33 1 L.M.1125.

naturally show a majority proportion of qualifying European works, limited enforcement and unequal application of the quota rule between Member States has limited any potential effect of the rule for such channels. Broadcasters would be expected to argue vociferously against quotas, but we have found that most confuse their real impact with the theoretical impact and also confuse the effect of national quotas with the *Television Without Frontiers* quotas. A number of broadcasters who we interviewed initially stated that quotas had had a significant impact on their business but were unable to identify specific examples. It became clear on further questioning of these broadcasters that it was domestic rules which were affecting decisions, not European quotas.[19]

In February 1996 the European Parliament (EP) voted to make the quota legally enforceable by removing the permissive 'wherever practicable' criteria for implementation. It also voted to extend these broadcast quotas to the new telecommunications services, thereby making on-line providers subject to them. The result of this would be to require, for example, over 50 per cent of the material in video on demand libraries to be of European origin. The EPs effort was however not successful as the 1997 amendments did not change the existing rules, and permit each Member State to grant exemptions on a case-by-case basis to the current requirement of 51 per cent EU-produced content. The amendments, moreover, allow greater flexibility for co-production of programming between European and non-European companies under 'bilateral co-production treaties'. Member States must also introduce a new definition of 'independent producer' to facilitate application of the rule requiring 10 per cent of transmission time or of programme budget to be reserved for independent productions.

The remainder of Chapter III of the original Directive (arts 7–9) was concerned with re-broadcasting of films (a continuing French worry, first raised by the erstwhile Minister of Culture, M. Jack Lang); language policy (stricter rules on the basis of language criteria were allowed); and purely local television. In the new Directive however, the periods for which cinematographic works may not be broadcast on television after first being shown in cinemas have been abolished. Member States are now merely required to ensure that the periods agreed between broadcasters and rights-holders

---

19. See *The Single Market Review Series, Subseries II – Impact on Services, Audio-Visual Services And Production*, KPMG, 1996.

are complied with. Article 8 on language policy has also been repealed.

The weightiest Chapter, Chapter IV, contains detailed provisions for the regulation of television advertising, extending over twelve Articles (arts 10–21), and has remained virtually unchanged. One of the main purposes of the Directive was the harmonizing of television advertising and sponsorship. It might be thought peculiar that, in a Directive which was supposed to promote a free market in programme services depending so significantly for financing on advertising, the Directive contains so many provisions concerning advertising and the interests of consumer protection and protection of morals and human dignity, for example, that subliminal techniques or surreptitious advertising are not to be used (art. 10). According to the Directive, television advertising must be readily recognizable as such and thus kept separate from other parts of the programme service by optical and/or acoustic means. Advertisements may be inserted during programmes, provided the integrity and value of the programme is not prejudiced. Natural breaks, such as the interval in a sports event, may be used for advertising slots. Feature films may be interrupted once for each period of 45 minutes. In other programmes, a period of a least 20 minutes should elapse between advertising breaks. There should be no breaks in the broadcasting of religious services, and none in news, current affairs, documentaries, religious or children's programmes, unless the programmes are of at least 30 minutes' duration (art. 11). Advertising shall not prejudice respect for human dignity and must not discriminate, be offensive, or be prejudicial to health, safety or the environment (art. 12). A number of prohibitions (tobacco products) and criteria for advertising (alcoholic beverages) are also specified. Particular regard must be had for minors (art. 16), and special requirements are laid down for sponsored programmes (art. 17). Total amounts of advertising per hour (20 per cent) and per day (15 per cent) are fixed and, again, Member States are free to lay down stricter provisions if they so wish. Public service messages and charity appeals are not to be included for the purposes of calculating these maximum periods. A definition of teleshopping has now also been introduced and is made subject to virtually the same rules as advertising. The former one-hour per day limit for teleshopping is abolished. Teleshopping channels are subject to most of the provisions of the Directive. Teleshopping windows on the generalist channels have to last at least 15 minutes and be clearly identifiable. They may not number more than eight per day and their total duration may not exceed three hours per day (art. 18). Teleshopping must not incite minors to conclude contracts for the purchase of goods or services.

Article 22 is for the general protection of minors and public order. Programmes which might seriously impair the development of minors are prohibited. Those which might simply be harmful to minors must, where they are not encrypted, be preceded by an acoustic warning or made clearly identifiable throughout their duration by means of a visual symbol. Broadcasts must not contain any incitement to hatred on grounds of race, sex, religion or nationality. The new Directive states also that within one year, the Commission is to submit a study of the advantages and disadvantages of other measures to facilitate parental control of broadcasts watched by their children, for example through use of the V-Chip.

Pornographic content remains one of the main anxieties in this area. In response to public concern that the *Television Without Frontiers* Directive might permit the free movement of programmes containing pornographic scenes, Mr Joao de Deus Pinheiro, the Commissioner responsible for audio-visual policy from 1993–94, made the following statement:

> Article 22 of the Directive provides for the protection of minors. Member States are required to take appropriate measures to ensure that broadcasts do not include programmes which might seriously impair the physical, mental or moral development of minors, in particular those that involve pornography or gratuitous violence. Such programmes are thus in principle not allowed. Nonetheless, the Directive, in accordance with the subsidiarity principle, is only applicable through Member States' legislation. The Member States retain the capacity to determine the means whereby this principle is to be respected, and have the responsibility in particular of defining the terms 'pornography' and 'might harm the development of minors', in accordance with their national moral standards. In the event that the broadcaster comes under the jurisdiction of the Member State which objects to the reception on its territory of such programmes, then that Member State clearly has, under the terms of the Directive, the possibility of acting against the broadcaster in question. In the case that the programmes are being transmitted by a broadcaster coming under another Member State's jurisdiction then the Directive expressly provides for a procedure whereby the Member State of reception can

exceptionally, under specific conditions monitored by the Commission, suspend such retransmission of the incriminated broadcasts on its territory. In fact, the infringement of art. 22 gives rise to the only exception to the principle of freedom of reception established by the Directive. In the light of these provisions, the Commission considers that it is quite clear that any Member State does have the possibility of acting against channels that might infringe art. 22 of the Directive, whether the broadcaster in question comes under its jurisdiction or not.[20]

Thus, as an exception,[21] from the general rule of freedom of reception and non-restriction of retransmission, art. 2a(2) of the Directive allows the Member States – provided that they respect a special procedure and only in exceptional circumstances – to take measures against broadcasters under the jurisdiction of another Member State who 'manifestly, seriously and gravely' infringe art. 22 of the Directive. This is designed to protect minors from programmes which could seriously impair their 'physical, mental or moral development'. The Member State concerned must notify the television broadcaster and the Commission in writing of the alleged infringements and the measures it intends to take if any such infringement occurs again, and consultations must be undertaken with the transmitting Member State and with the Commission. If they do not produce an amicable settlement within 15 days of the notification, and the alleged infringement persists, the receiving Member State may take unilateral provisional measures against the channel concerned. The Commission is to ensure that the measures taken should be compatible with Community law. If it decides that they are not, it may require the Member State to put an end to the measures in question as a matter of urgency. So far only the United Kingdom has felt it necessary to have recourse – at least three times – to this procedure. In the first two cases (the '*Rendez-Vous Télévision*' case and the '*XXXTV*' case), the consultations did not produce a settlement and the British authorities considered it necessary to adopt a prohibition order against the channels under the jurisdiction of another Member State. Following contacts with

[20.] In *Europe Without Frontiers*, ch. 6 'Freedom to Provide Services'. Available at <http://europa.eu.int/en/comm/dg10/infcom/xc5/ewfqa/index.htm>

[21.] For a more detailed discussion of the application of article 22 see *2nd Report from the Commission to the European Parliament, the Council and the Economic and Social Committee on the application of the Directive 89/552/EEC, Television without Frontiers* (1997), pages 6–8.

the Member States concerned and after considering the effects of the measures communicated by the United Kingdom, the Commission considered in both cases that these measures were compatible with Community law. This judgment was largely based on a test of proportionality and on an assessment of the possible discriminatory effects of the measures.[22] It is also important to highlight the fact that, in the system of Community rules created by the Directive (art 2(1)), Member States are not permitted to apply discriminatory moral criteria to the broadcasters under their jurisdiction: a stricter attitude to programmes to be received in their territory and a more lenient attitude to programmes destined to be broadcast abroad (typically, satellite channel programmes) would not be acceptable. On the contrary, the Member States are bound to ensure that all the broadcasters under their jurisdiction comply with art. 22.

Article 23 prescribes that there be a right of reply, but leaves a wide measure of discretion to Member States as to how it should be established and implemented. However the provisions relating to the right of reply of parties whose reputation and good name have been damaged by an assertion of incorrect facts in a television programme have now been strengthened in a new art. 23 which imposes some restrictions on the discretion of Member States and, for example, requires that the reply must be within a reasonable time and in an appropriate manner.

Application of the Directive is the responsibility of each Member State's national authorities responsible for regulating the audio-visual industry. Systematic contact with the national bodies was maintained, particularly through the *ad hoc* group of representatives of the Member States, set up within the Commission on the latter's initiative. This work of the *ad hoc* group has staked out a path for the future work of the 'Contact Committee' which has now been set up by art. 23a of the 1997 Directive. Specifically, the Committee, which is chaired by the Commission and composed of representatives of the authorities of the Member States will have to:

- facilitate the effective implementation of the Directive by organizing regular consultations on all the practical problems arising from its application, in particular the application of art. 2, and on other topics on which discussions seem useful;

22. See Commission opinions C(96) 3933 final in the 'Rendez-Vous Télévision' case and C(95)2678 final in the 'XXXTV' case.

- give opinions – on its own initiative or at the request of the Commission – on the application by the Member States of the provisions of the Directive;

- act as a forum for the exchange of views on topics to be addressed in the reports that the Member States must provide pursuant to art. 4(3), on their methods, on the mandate of the independent study required on labelling techniques, on the assessment of offers relating to it and on this study itself;

- discuss the results of the regular consultations that the Commission holds with representatives of associations of broadcasters, producers, consumers, manufacturers, service providers, trade unions and the artistic community;

- facilitate the exchange of information between the Member States and the Commission on the situation and development of legislation in the field of television broadcasting, taking into account the audio-visual policy pursued by the Community and the relevant developments in the technical field; and

- examine any development in the sector for which consultation would appear useful.

Caselaw of the European Court of Justice[23]

The Court of Justice has given several judgments on the scope and interpretation of the 1989 Directive. Most of the Court's decisions, whether in proceedings for failure to fulfil an obligation under Community law on the Commission's initiative (art. 169 EC), or in a preliminary ruling case (art 177 EC), mainly apply to the various aspects of the system of the division of competences between Member States for broadcasters in Europe, and especially to the criteria for legal jurisdiction. The specific topics that the Court has examined in its judgments to date are:[24] the extent of the originating country's jurisdiction and the criteria for bringing broad-

[23.] Based upon *2nd Report from the Commission to the European Parliament, the Council and the Economic and Social Committee on the application of the Directive 89/552/EEC, Television without Frontiers* (1997), pages 9–19. For a further discussion of some specific cases see: in Mortelmans (K.) and Temmink (H.), Europese rechtspraak over de TV Richtlijn. In: *MediaForum*, November/December 1996, pp. 138–145 and Dehousse (F.), La politique europeenne de l'audiovisuel. In *Courrier Hebdomadaire* CRISP, 1996, n 1525–1526.

[24.] See *Second Report from the Commission to the European Parliament, the Council and the Economic and Social Committee on the application of Directive 89/552/EEC 'Television without Frontiers'* (1997).

casters under its legal system, the possibility of Member States adopting more stringent or more detailed rules to apply to broadcasters under their jurisdiction, and the powers of the receiving Member State in terms of programmes transmitted from other Member States.

It is important to stress that the positions taken by the Court supplement the choices made by the Community in adopting the 1997 Directive (see above). Certain amendments made by the new Directive in fact aim to clarify the text in the light of the Court's rulings. Far from losing its importance after the amendments to the *Television Without Frontiers* Directive have been adopted, the case law of the Court shown below will therefore maintain its value.[25]

Case C-412/93 Leclerc-Siplec, 9 February 1995[26]

The *Leclerc-Siplec* judgment of 9 February 1995 was the first case of judicial application of the *Television Without Frontiers* Directive. It concerned a complaint lodged by Leclerc-Siplec against the refusal of TF1 and M6 to broadcast an advertisement concerning the distribution of fuel in Leclerc supermarkets, in accordance with French law. The matter was referred for a preliminary ruling to the Court, which ruled that arts. 30, 85, 86 and 3 of the EC Treaty, and the provisions of the Directive, did not preclude the Member States from prohibiting the broadcasting of advertisements for the distribution sector by television broadcasters established on their territory. This judgment clarifies the relationship between arts 3, 19 and 20 of the Directive. According to the Court, art. 19 simply clarifies a general freedom conferred on the Member States by art. 3(1), to lay down more detailed or stricter rules as regards television broadcasters under their jurisdiction (it should be noted that the 1997 Directive abrogates art. 19 of the 1989 Directive). Article

---

[25.] At the time of writing, the European Commission decided to bring an action in the Court of Justice for a declaration that the Italian Republic has failed to fulfil its obligations under the EC Treaty and the *Television Without Frontiers* Directive. The decision is the culmination of infringement proceedings (an art 169 letter was sent on 15 January 1996 and a reasoned opinion followed on 7 August 1997) relating to Italy's incorrect transposal of certain provisions of the Directive on television services, particularly the rules governing interruption of programmes for advertising slots and the promotion of European productions. See *Press Release IP/97/1154*, Brussels, 18 December 1997.

[26.] [1995] 1 ECR 179.

20, on the other hand, allows them to lay down less strict rules than those in art. 11(2)–(5) and art. 18 for programmes which are intended only for the national territory and which may not be received, directly or indirectly, in one or more other Member States. The Court's interpretation gives the Member States, subject to compliance with the rules of the Treaty (which in this case were considered to have been complied with) and those of freedom of reception and retransmission of channels under the jurisdiction of other Member States, a broad margin for assessment of the interests which could justify stricter or more detailed measures than those in the Directive.

Case C-222/94, Commission v United Kingdom and C-11/95, Commission v Belgium, 10 September 1996[27]

Here the Court had the opportunity to pursue a general reflection on the Directive. It made a major contribution to the definition of its scope, to the clarification of the concept of 'jurisdiction', and to the application of the principle of the 'place of establishment' of the intra-Community television broadcasters (see above).

In Case C-222/94 (*Commission v United Kingdom*), the Court gave a detailed interpretation of art. 2. The principal point at issue was the definition of the reasons for which a Member State must assert its jurisdiction over a given broadcasting organisation.[28] As there is no specific provision in the Directive, the Commission has always recommended applying the principle of the place of establishment. The Court's interpretation of art. 2(1) leads to the conclusion that the concept of jurisdiction of a Member State must be understood as necessarily covering jurisdiction over television broadcasters, which can be based only on the broadcaster's connection to that State's legal system. This last concept finds practical expression in the concept of establishment as used in the first paragraph of art. 59 of the EC Treaty. The adoption by a Member State of the EU of any criterion other than that of the place of establishment, and particularly that of the place of the initial transmission or the target audience, may lead that state to carry out a 'double check' on broadcasters which already come under the

27. [1996] ECR I-4025; [1996] ECR I-3143.
28. For a discussion see 1997 581 HC Debs, cols. 559–63 (8 July 1997). This decision led to the adoption of the Satellite Television Service Regulations 1997 in the UK (SI No 1682).

jurisdiction of another Member State or, by contrast, to fail to ensure the application of its legislation to all the broadcasters which
come under its jurisdiction. As a result of this interpretation, certain parts of UK law have been declared to be not in conformity
with arts 2 and 3(2) of the Directive.

The second decision (*Commission v Belgium*) poses the basic
question of the compatibility with Community law of a general
system of conditional prior authorization for the retransmission of
television programmes coming under the jurisdiction of another
Member State. The Commission considered that the need for prior
authorization granted by the authorities in the receiving country,
on condition that the broadcasters met various conditions (such as,
in the case of the French Community in Belgium, the conclusion of
agreements specifying cultural obligations with the Executive,
which may in all cases be revoked), constituted a serious restriction on the retransmission of television broadcasts from other
Member States, and that it contravened art. 2(2) of the Directive.
The Belgian Government invoked several arguments to justify put-
ting such a system in place. First, regarding the French Community's provisions on cable television, it alleged that cable
retransmission did not come within the scope of the Directive. The
Court, however, considered that the ninth and tenth recitals and
arts 1(a) and 2(2) led to the conclusion that the Directive did, effectively, concern cable retransmission of television programmes.
The other arguments presented aimed to assert the right of the receiving Member States to exercise a certain form of control ('sec-
ondary control') on televised programmes emanating from other
Member States. Reasons given were, for example, the need to
check whether a broadcaster has the right to enjoy the freedoms
guaranteed by the Treaty and, if so, under the jurisdiction of
which Member State; safeguarding pluralism in the media; protection of copyright; and the need to ensure respect for public policy
and morality. The Court clearly stated that the Belgian Government had not shown that the protection of such interests was such
as to justify a general system of prior authorization for programmes emanating from other Member States, which involves a
de facto abolition of the freedom to provide services.

Cases C-14/96 Paul Denuit of 29 May 1997 and C-56/96 VT4 of 5 June 1997[29]

The Court confirmed the earlier case law in these two judgments and developed it further. In Case C-14/96, the Belgian authorities (French Community) refused permission for the cable distributor, Coditel Brabant, to distribute programmes of a broadcaster under British jurisdiction (TNT/Cartoon) on the ground that it did not comply with the Directive, particularly those provisions relating to the promotion of European works (arts 4 and 5). The Court had already partially answered the questions raised in its judgments of 10 September 1996 (see above), but in this case, the Belgian authorities also considered that TNT/Cartoon programmes did not come under the jurisdiction of a Member State within the meaning of art. 2(1) of the *Television Without Frontiers* Directive because they did not fulfil the requirements of arts 4 and 5 (broadcasting quotas) and that, in fact, most of the broadcaster's programming emanated from a country that was not a Member State of the European Community. The Court stated quite clearly that 'a television broadcaster comes under the jurisdiction of the Member State in which it is established. The origin of programmes broadcast by the television broadcaster or their conformity with arts 4 and 5 of the Directive are irrelevant in determining the Member State having jurisdiction over such a broadcaster pursuant to art. 2(1).'

In Case C-56/96, the Belgian authorities (Flemish Community) refused to authorize the Flemish cable networks to distribute the programmes of VT4, a broadcaster established in the United Kingdom. Referring to the TV10 judgment of 5 October 1994 (Case C-23/93), the Flemish Minister of Culture considered that VT4, whose activities were totally or principally aimed at the Flemish Community, was trying to circumvent the Flemish law. VT4, however, referred to art. 2 of the Directive, according to which the receiving State does not have the right to refuse access to its national cable network if the foreign broadcasting organization is licensed by another Member State. In its judgment, the Court considered, first, that the fact that all VT4's programmes and advertising are exclusively intended for the Flemish public did not in itself show that VT4 cannot be considered as being established in the United Kingdom. Secondly, it confirms and clarifies its ruling in the *Commission v United Kingdom* case cited above by deciding that when

29. [1997] ECR I-2785; [1997] ECR I-3143.

a television broadcaster is established in a Member State, jurisdiction over it is exercised by the Member State in whose territory the broadcaster has the centre of its activities. Thus, even if all the programmes of a broadcaster from a Member State were conceived and intended exclusively for the public in another Member State, only the originating Member State may examine their compatibility with its national law (including the provisions implementing the Directive).

Case C-320/94 et al. (RTI) of 12 December 1996[30]

The Regional Administrative Court for Lazio (Italy) had made several requests to the Court of Justice, under art. 177 of the EC Treaty, for preliminary rulings interpreting the Directive, notably regarding sponsorship and 'telepromotions' (a common form of television advertising in Italy, based on the interruption of studio programmes, especially game shows, by slots devoted to the presentation of one or more products or services, where the programme presenters momentarily swap their role in the games in progress for one as 'promoters' of the goods or services which are the object of the advertising presentation). The questions essentially concerned the interpretation of arts 17(1)(b) and 18 of the Directive. The Court decided that art. 17(1)(b) of the Directive must be interpreted as meaning that it does not prohibit references to the name and/or logo of the sponsor at moments other than the beginning and/or end of the sponsored programme; and arts 1(b) and 18 of the Directive must be interpreted in the sense that the expression 'forms of advertisements such as direct offers to the public', used in art. 18, is used by way of example. Consequently, other forms of advertising which share with teleshopping ('direct offers') the characteristic of lasting longer than spot advertisements (such as 'telepromotions'), may be included for the purposes of extending from 15 per cent to 20 per cent the daily limit of time devoted to television advertising. Under the new Directive all forms of advertising are subject to a new daily maximum limit and the expression 'forms of advertisements such as direct offers to the

30. *Reti Televisive Italiane SpA (RTI)* (C-320/94), *Radio Torre* (C-328/94), *Rete A Srl* (C-329/94), *Vallau Italiana Promomarket Srl* (C-337/94), *Radio Italia Solo Musica Srl e.a.* (C-338/94) and *GETE Srl* (C-339/94) *v Ministero delle Poste e Telecommunicazioni* Joined Cases C-320/94, C-328/94, C-329/94, C-337/94, C-338/94 and C-339/94, [1997] 1 CMLR 346.

public' has been deleted. The daily limit of one hour of teleshopping (art 18(3)) has also been deleted and replaced by new provisions tailored to both generalist channels and channels exclusively devoted to teleshopping.

Cases C-34, C-35, C-36/95 De Agostini and TV-Shop, 11 June, 17 September 1996, 9 July 1997[31]

In Joined Cases C-34, C-35 and C-36/95 (*Konsumentombudsmannen v*, respectively, *De Agostini Svenska Förlad AB and TV-Shop I Sverige* AB) advertising and teleshopping programmes received in Sweden were considered by the *Konsumentombudsman* (Consumer Ombudsman) to be unfair under the Trading Practices Act,[32] either because they directly targetted children (Case C-34/95), as Swedish law prohibits advertising programmes aimed at children under 12 years of age, or for other reasons (particularly those connected with the clarity, precision and exhaustiveness of the advertisements) they were potentially harmful to consumers' interests. The court hearing the three cases (the *Marknadsdomstol* of Stockholm) decided to refer one question in each of them to the EFTA Court. Following Sweden's accession to the EC Treaty, the proceedings were transferred to the Court of Justice in Luxembourg. The main subject of the case was the application of the Swedish national law regarding misleading advertising and televised advertising aimed at children under 12 years of age in two cases where Swedish advertisers were transmitting their advertising messages to the Swedish public. In the three cases, the televised advertising in question was transmitted by a broadcaster under the jurisdiction of another Member State (TV3 – UK) and, at the same time, by broadcasters under Swedish jurisdiction (TV4 in Case C-34/95 and Homeshopping Channel in Cases C-35/95 and C-36/95). The Court, in its judgment of 9 July 1997, first notes that fair trading and the protection of consumers in general are overriding requirements of general public importance which may justify – under certain conditions – obstacles to the free movement of goods and the free provision of services. In the case of television advertising, compliance with the provisions in the Directive to protect minors must be ensured by the broadcasting State alone. Consequently, the receiving State may no longer apply to programmes

---

31. [1997] All ER (EC) 687.   32. Marknadsföringslagen 1975:1418.

emanating from another Member State provisions specifically designed to control the content of television advertising with regard to minors. However, art. 3 of the Directive allows Member States to apply stricter rules to the broadcasters under their jurisdiction. In order to assess the compatibility of Swedish law with arts 30 and 59 of the EC Treaty in the case in question, the Court considered that it was for the national court to check whether the national provisions were actually necessary to meet overriding requirements of general public importance or one of the aims laid down in arts 36 and 56 of the Treaty, whether they were proportionate for that purpose and whether the aims or overriding requirements could have been met by less restrictive means.

CHAPTER SIX

Other Legal Measures and Support Mechanisms

Satellite and Cable

The basic framework provided by the *Television Without Frontiers* Directive is supplemented in various other fields to ensure the effective free circulation of the services by other legal instruments in the area of delivery systems as described below.

In the satellite field,[1] the Community adopted several directives to foster a harmonized and liberalized market. The reasoning behind those directives was developed in the 1990 Satellite Green Paper and consequent Council Resolution of 1991.[2] In the run-up to the Single Market, four main lines of action were proposed:

1) full liberalization of the terrestrial sector, but with regulatory mechanisms safeguarding specific interests;
2) harmonization of the provision of services, by mutual recognition of national licensing procedures;
3) ensuring free access to the capacity of the space sector on a fair, non-discriminatory basis and according to costs, subject to exclusive rights or measures taken by the Member States;
4) complete commercial freedom for suppliers in the space sector, in particular for the direct marketing of space segment capacity to service providers and users.

The first reflection of this principle was in the 1988 Terminal Equipment Directive[3] which required Member States to eliminate the licensing of consumer reception antennae. The 1994 Satellite

---

1. See, White S., Bate S. and Johnson T., *Satellite Communications in Europe: Law and Regulation.* (FT Law & Tax, 1996), pp. 145–216.
2. OJ No C 8, 14. 1. 1992.
3. Commission Directive of 16 May 1988 on competition in the markets in telecommunications terminal equipment (88/301 /EEC).

Services Directive[4] provided for an open market in the use of satellite telecommunications facilities, including uplink stations used to transport broadcast signals. Finally, the April 1997 Licensing Directive[5] was adopted to provide a common structure for licensing all telecommunications facilities, again including satellite facilities and services, but not the activity of providing broadcast programming to consumers, which is regulated in the *Television Without Frontiers* Directive. Moreover it is important to underline that the European Community considers a strong and coherent satellite communications industry and services sector of high economic and political importance. Therefore the Commission decided in a Communication[6] on satellite communications to take a more proactive and consistent approach in this area. For example, one step in the proposed Action Plan was to request industry to identify regulatory barriers, allowing the Commission to formulate regulatory measures needed in the satellite communications sector, as well as to report on the effectiveness of the measures taken to date.

Since 1 January 1996, all cable television networks have also been allowed to provide all liberalized telecommunications services in the European Community, including home banking, interactive video games, TV shopping and on-line databases. Basic voice telephony services were opened to cable companies on 1 January 1998, the date proposed by the Green Paper on telecoms infrastructure liberalization[7] for opening voice telephony to full competition. The debate[8] held before the adoption of the Directive[9] partly concentrated on cross-ownership of telecommunications and cable TV networks. The Directive required that Member

---

4. Commission Directive 94/46/EC of 13 October 1994 amending Directive 88/301/EEC and Directive 90/388/EEC in particular with regard to satellite communications.
5. Directive 97/13/EC, OJ 1997 L117/15.   6. COM(97)91 final, 5 March 1997
7. *Green paper on a common approach to the liberalization of telecommunications infrastructure and cable television networks – Part One: Principle and Timetable*, COM(94)440 final, 25 October 1994. The cornerstone of the liberalization of telecommunications services was the Commission's Services Directive 90/388/EEC of 28 June 1990, OJEC L192/10, 24 July 1990 (see further Chapter Seven below).
8. There was pressure from various Member States to withdraw this initiative. See van Eijk, N., 'Liberalisation of Cable Television Networks in Europe'. In *IRIS 1995: Legal Developments in the Audio-visual Sector*, pp. 17–19.
9. Commission Directive 95/51/EC of 18 October 1995 amending Directive 90/388/EEC with regard to the abolition of the restrictions on the use of cable television networks for the provision of already liberalized telecommunications services, OJEC No L 256:49–54, 26 October 1995.

States impose regulations to ensure transparent accounting and non-discriminatory behaviour where an operator has the exclusive right to provide the infrastructure for public telecommunications networks and also provides the infrastructure for cable TV networks. The underlying rationale behind the Directive is based on 'symmetry' of liberalization: once cable operators may enter the telecoms services market, then telecom operators may enter the TV broadcasting market and vice versa. The 1995 Cable Directive and the 1996 Full Liberalization Directive required however the Commission to review the Cable Directive from two particular points of view: the impact on competition of the joint provision of telecommunications and cable TV networks by a single operator; and the restrictions on the use of telecommunication networks for the provision of cable TV capacity. In its so-called Cable Review[10] the Commission concluded that accounting separation in the case of joint provision of competing networks by dominant telecommunication operators, as established by the Commission Cable Directive, has been shown to be insufficient to facilitate pro-competitive development in the multimedia sector. Minimum steps should include *inter alia* the effective separation of these operators from their cable TV network companies, i.e. the operation of these activities by clearly separated legal entities. Further action by the Commission would be justified with regard to specific cases to reduce the anti-competitive effect of dominant positions reinforced by the joint provision of both types of networks by one and the same operator, a situation inherited from previous legally protected monopoly positions.

Not all regulation in these areas is however undertaken through Community Directives. In other areas connected with broadcasting, the Member States retain the right to legislate in respect of Community law. In these areas, the application of art. 59 of the Treaty, which provides for the abolition of obstacles to the freedom to provide services, makes it possible to prevent new violations of the European audio-visual area. Finally, the satisfactory functioning of a European audio-visual area presupposes the maintenance of an open market and effective competition, and therefore virtually all such economic activity is subject to EU competition law, which is also discussed further below.

10. *Commission communication concerning the review under competition rules of the joint provision of telecommunications and cable TV networks by a single operator and the abolition of restrictions on the provision of cable TV capacity over telecommunications*, SEC(97)2390.

Content regulation in newer audio-visual services

Two major actions have been undertaken by the Commission dealing with content and the newer services. Firstly, a Communication on harmful and illegal content on the Internet was issued in November 1996.[11] The Communication refers to the legal and regulatory challenges posed by content circulating on the Internet, giving particular emphasis on the issue of harmful and illegal content. It proposes options for short term action to combat or control such content, such as self-regulation, technical protection, improved international cooperation, education and awareness. Secondly, the Green Paper on the protection of Minors and Human Dignity in Audio-visual and Information Services initiated a medium- to long-term reflection on these issues.[12] Following consultations on these communications, the European Commission has firstly adopted an Action Plan[13] for 1998 to 2001 on promoting the safe use of the Internet, which identifies key areas where measures are needed and could be supported by the European Union. This concerns in particular a hot line on which Internet users could report allegedly illegal content; industry-led self-regulation and content-monitoring schemes; and internationally compatible and interoperable rating and filtering systems. Secondly, the Commission also adopted a draft Council Recommendation on the protection of minors and of human dignity in audio-visual services. The underlying idea is that self-regulation schemes at national level are the most appropriate answer as regards both television and the Internet.

Support actions for the programme industry

The strengthening of the programme industry and the desire to make it more competitive have been a fundamental objective of Community audio-visual policy right from the outset, as described in Chapter Four. The principal support instruments are the MEDIA Programmes[14] based on art. 235 EC, and effectively supplementing efforts made at national level. To comply with the

---

11. COM (96)487.   12. COM (96)483.
13. <http://www2.echo.lu/legal/en/internet/actplan.html>
14. The MEDIA Programme was set up by Council Decision 90/685/EEC, of 21 December 1990, relating to the implementation of an action programme to encourage the development of the European audio-visual industry (MEDIA 1991–95). This programme was reshaped into a MEDIA II programme based

principle of subsidiarity, they relate to structural objectives having a direct and indirect impact, both on the production of European works and on their circulation in the Member States. Similarly, the European Guarantee Fund for the audio-visual sphere is aimed at creating a financial instrument capable of mobilizing investment in the European audio-visual programme industry. Given that their principal objective is to promote the development of the programme industry, MEDIA II and the guarantee fund are based on art. 130 (industry) of the EC Treaty. However, these instruments also take full account of the cultural aspects of the industrial sector they intend to promote, as is the intention of art. 128 (culture), paragraph 4. What follows is a brief discussion of those initiatives.

The MEDIA programme is a European Commission initiative which provides and streamlines funding and other support to develop the European audio-visual industry. An experimental phase was launched under the acronym MEDIA92 in 1988, as detailed in Chapter Four. It was financed from the Commission's own resources and therefore did not require the assent of the Council. Subsequently, in December 1990, the Council of Ministers was able to adopt it as a fully fledged five-year programme. Renamed MEDIA95, it was given a budget of ECU 200 million. At the beginning of 1996, MEDIAII came into force. It is designed to promote the European audio-visual industry[15] over the next six years and it operates on the basis of loans or subsidies. The budget has been set at ECU 310 million (instead of the proposed 400 million).[16] The new focus of MEDIAII follows the industry consultation process which took place after the Green Paper on Audio-visual Policy. It focuses on three 'priority areas', grouping about 20 more detailed lines of action;[17]

14. (Continued) on two Council Decisions, firstly No. 95/563/EC, relating to a programme to encourage the development and the dissemination of European audio-visual works (MEDIA II – Development and dissemination) (1996–2000) and, secondly, No. 95/564/EC, relating to a training programme for professionals in the European audio-visual programme industry (MEDIA II – training) (1996–2000).

15. The programme will also be open to associate Central and Eastern European countries (for example, Romania's audio-visual sector will be able to take part in the programme from 1/1/1997), EEA countries, Cyprus and Malta and other countries with relevant cooperation agreements with the European Union.

16. Germany, the Netherlands and the UK blocked the French and European Commission ambitions to double the budget of the MEDIA programme from ECU 200 million to ECU 400 million.

17. See, MEDIA II, The Union's support mechanism for the European audio-visual industry. At: <http://europa.eu.int/en/comm/dg10/avpolicy/media/en/home-m2.htmln>

- the training of European professionals.[18] The training programme (ECU 45 million) aims to develop awareness of economic and commercial management skills as well as encouraging the use of new technologies for the production of programmes;
- the development of (pre-)production projects aimed at the European and world markets. It will address three main aspects of the development stage, namely screenplay writing, financial engineering for productions and marketing;
- the transnational distribution of European films and television programmes (ECU 265 million for development and distribution).[19]

The ability of MEDIA II to fulfil its aim of boosting the competitiveness of the European audio-visual industry has been questioned. According to the industry[20] the content of MEDIA II is 'confused and incomprehensible', and the budgets are insufficient to meet the demands of the industry. The budget is also out of proportion to the funds available for the promotion of hardware, e.g. for HDTV which have been much higher (see below).[21]

However, to complement the MEDIA II programme, the European Commission published in November 1995 a proposal[22] for a Council Decision setting up a European Guarantee Fund. The latter was approved by the European Parliament in October 1996[23] and is at the time of writing being discussed at the Council. The fund (ECU 200 million) will be targeted at European cinema and

---

18. Council Decision of 22 December 1995 on the implementation of a training programme for professionals in the European audio-visual programme industry (Media II – Training), OJEC No L321, 30 December 1995, pp. 33–8.
19. Council Decision of 10 July 1995 on the implementation of a programme encouraging the development and distribution of European audio-visual works, OJEC No L 321, 30 December 1995, pp. 25–32.
20. *Joint position of Committee of Cinematographic Industries of the EU (CICCE), the Producers' Association and the European Federation of Audio-visual Producers (FERA).* (Agence Europe, 11 August 1995).
21. See, Burgelman J.C. and Pauwels C., 'La convergence de l'audiovisuel et des telecommunications en Europe' in *La politique des Communautés Européennes*, Lentic, 1990.
22. *Proposal of the European Commission for a Council Decision establishing a European Guarantee Fund to promote cinema and television production*, COM(95)546 final, 14 November 1995.
23. *Proposal for a Council Decision establishing a European Guarantee Fund to promote cinema and television production and legislative resolution embodying Parliament's opinion on the proposal.* European Parliament, Minutes of the Sitting of Tuesday, 22 October 1996, Provisional Edition, PE 252.722: 12–21.

television companies. It will not finance projects directly, since it will work as an insurer, offering financial institutions the opportunity to share the risks associated with financial operations in this area by granting them partial guarantees on loans and credit. It is proposed to place the fund under the management structures of the European Investment Fund (EIF). The proposal was welcomed by the industry[24] and was approved by the European Parliament[25] in October 1996. However some Member States (especially the UK, the Netherlands and Germany) opposed the project at several EU Council Meetings.[26] ECOSOC also expressed the need to examine the proposal in more detail.[27] The proposal will therefore be discussed again. The Fund management plan is prepared by the Commission, as well as a list of the financial institutions said to be interested in taking part.

Meanwhile Audio-visual Eureka (AVE) has redefined its mission in its London Declaration,[28] which came into effect from 1 January 1996. AVE is a pan-European initiative also aimed at strengthening the European audio-visual industry. It was established in 1989 as a result of an initiative of the French Government and was partly modelled on the Research and Technology Eureka programme. There are 34 participating members, including all Member States of the EU and the European Economic Area (EEA) and most of the central and eastern European countries and the Baltic States. The declaration follows an independent evaluation of

24. The European Film Companies Alliance (EFCA), a body representing seven major EU production companies, was pleased that such funding will generate investment in the audio-visual sector. Brussels:Agence Europe, 29/11/95.

25. Burgelman and Pauwels, *op. cit.*

26. At the 2022nd Council meeting – Audiovisual/Cultural Affairs in Luxembourg, 30 June 1997, the majority of delegations reiterated their support for such a Guarantee Fund. The proposal is based on a Treaty article which requires a unanimous Council decision (art. 130s concerning Industry). The draft currently on the table is basically still the compromise presented by the Irish Presidency last autumn and discussed during the Council meeting of 16 December 1996. See DN: PRES/97/221, 1997-07-07. The major reservations can be summarized in three reasons: lack of clarity concerning the proposed agreement between the Commission and the EIF; scepticism as to the Fund's financial self-sufficiency and the need to say more on the position of small and medium-sized companies. See, *IRIS,* July 1997, Vol. II, No. 7, p. 12.

27. *Opinion of the Economic and Social Committee on the 'Proposal for a Council Decision establishing a European Guarantee Fund to promote cinema and television production'.* OJ No C 204: 5–8, 15 July 1996.

28. See, *Audio-visual Eureka initiative is refocused under the UK's presidency.* London: Department of National Heritage, press release 224/95, 30 November 1995.

AVE and established new objectives.[29] AVE has decided to concentrate, through a four-year programme, on the same priorities of the MEDIA II programme, namely training, development and distribution. Also within AVE, it is important to mention the existence of the European Audio-visual Observatory, which collects and disseminates information on technical, legal and market data; this has been described with the Council of Europe in Chapter Three.

Finally, under the terms of the European Audiovisual Dimension, the support given to prizes and festivals traditionally makes it possible to provide financial support for audio-visual festivals, particularly cinema, by programming quality European works. This action, developed since 1992, has a threefold objective: 'it enables European works to be promoted; it favours their circulation and their distribution (whereas, in the case of each Member State, only a very small part of nationally-produced films is the subject of programming in other Member States); and it facilitates mutual awareness of national film industries'.[30]

The MAC legacy and standardization

In addition to the preoccupation of the European Community with promotion of the programme industry, an increased interest and activity can be seen in the field of transmission standards after the high definition television (HDTV) failure. The mobilization of resources in favour of HDTV must be seen in the context of the European attempt to revive the European consumer electronics industry. The rationale was that a European HDTV standard would provide a defensive screen behind which the Community's electronics industries could shelter from Japanese (and United States) competition and give them early, and protected, access to what was believed would become a very large market. The European HDTV project was established as EU95 under the umbrella of the Eureka Programme by a group of leading European consumer electronics companies including Bosch, Philips, Thomson and Thorn EMI. Although the plan was essentially a Eureka project, the European Commission and especially DGXIII had

---

29. See, 1996 Action Plan at <http://www.aveureka.be/>
30. See <http://europa.eu.int/en/comm/dg10/avpolicy/avpolicy.html>

invested political as well as financial capital in it. The policy was ultimately doomed, as digital technology and commercial broadcasters' actions undermined its viability and the European Commission (DGXIII) continued beyond the point at which failure was unavoidable. This failure however proved less damaging to the firms than to DGXIII, whose HDTV strategy and regulatory initiatives was designed almost exclusively to foster EU95. The Commission's political credibility was put at risk, and in the reshuffle of responsibilities in 1993 DGXIII was severely weakened.[31]

In May 1992, a Directive[32] (the so-called MAC Directive) was issued requiring the use of D2-MAC for all new non-digital satellite channels launched after 1st January 1995. The Commission had proposed, as part of its attempt to promote HDTV, adopting an interim standard known as D2-MAC, developed by the EU95 HDTV Consortium, which was part of the research and technology Eureka project (see above). The Directive formed part of the promotion and it included a package of financial support which was to be offered to assist programme production and broadcasting in the new standard. However, the financial package was blocked by the UK and this resulted in the Commission re-examining its strategy and adopting a new approach aimed at promoting new wide-screen and high definition television technologies without recommending particular technological solutions.

Its *Decision for an Action Plan on the introduction of advanced television services in Europe*[33] has as its objective to accelerate the development of advanced television services in the 16:9 wide screen format on 625 or 1,250 line services, regardless of the standard used and irrespective of the broadcasting mode (terrestrial, satellite or cable). The Action Plan ran to the end of June 1997 and aimed through funding specific projects to encourage television channels to make a critical mass of programmes in 16:9 format in order to optimize audiences and to encourage consumers to buy the new large screen televisions. At present a total number of 39 broadcasters transmitting in 13 Member States are funded.[34]

---

31. See, Dai X., Cawson A. and Holmes P., 'The Rise and Fall of High Definition Television: The Impact of European Technology Policy', in *Journal of Common Market Studies*, June 1996, Vol. 34, No. 2, pp. 149–166.

32. Council Directive 92/38/EEC of 11 May 1992 on the adoption of standards for Satellite Broadcasting of Television Signals, OJEC No L137:17, 20 May 1992.

33. Council Decision 93/424/EEC of 22 July 1993, OJEC No L196:48, 5 August 1993.

34. Their 50,000 hours of wide-screen broadcasting have triggered sales of 500,000 16:9 TV sets so far, with a 64 per cent increase in 1995 alone. The format is

The re-examination of the 'MAC Directive' resulted also in the adoption on 24 October 1995 of the *Directive on the use of standards for the transmission of television signals.*[35] The Directive promotes and harmonizes accelerated development of advanced television services, wide screen 16:9 format, HDTV and digital transmission systems. Access to digital-pay TV (or conditional access) is tackled by a dual approach promoting the use of a common interface for digital encryption, but still allows for proprietary systems provided that 'gatekeepers' grant licences for the use of such systems to broadcasters on a non-discriminatory basis. It does however not target the introduction of particular services and technologies, preferring a studied neutrality across the board. The final text seems to be very much influenced by lobbying from the Digital Video Broadcasting group (DVB).[36] National implementation of the Directive however varies considerably and could lead to both technical (rival systems) and regulatory fragmentation; a review has been called for, and we shall return to this issue in our discussion of competition law below.

Meanwhile, in 1996 the Commission published a *Green Paper on legal protection for encrypted services,*[37] noting that the absence of harmonized regulation is holding back the development of a Single European Market in encrypted services. The Green Paper formed the basis for wide-ranging consultations and a proposed Directive[38] by the Commission on legal protection of television and radio broadcasting and information society services, offered to the public at a distance where access is subject to payment. Such services include pay-TV, video-on-demand, music-on-demand,

34. (*Continued*) strongest in Germany, France and Belgium, with Denmark, Greece, Italy, Sweden and Austria following as new markets in 1995. *News from the Spokesman's midday briefing*, 05/09/1996 at: <http://europa.eu.int/en/comm/spp/me/midday.html>

35. Directive 95/47/EC of the European Parliament and of the Council of 24 October 1995 on the use of standards for the transmission of television signals, OJEC, No L 281:51–54, 23 November 1995.

36. DVB is a consortium of more than 140 European manufactures, broadcasters and programme makers. See, Watson A., 'Mutual recognition of licences for satellite broadcasting and regulatory framework for digital television.' in: *IRIS 1995: Legal Developments in the Audio-visual Sector*, p. 22.

37. COM(96)0076.

38. Communication From The Commission To The European Parliament, The Council And The Economic And Social Committee, *Proposal For A European Parliament And Council Directive on the Legal Protection of Services based on, or consisting of, Conditional Access* (presented by the Commission), prov. version, 9 July 1997, COM (97)0356 (final).

electronic publishing, etc. If adopted by the Council of Ministers and the European Parliament under the co-decision procedure, the Directive will require Member States to prohibit, and to provide appropriate sanctions against, all commercial activities related to unauthorized access to a protected service, such as the sale of pirate decoders, smart-cards or software. It will also prohibit Member States from invoking 'anti-piracy' grounds to restrict the free movement of legitimate services and conditional access devices originating in another Member State. The proposal does not address the use of encryption for security or confidentiality reasons, (which is discussed in the Communication of the Commission *Towards A European Framework for Digital Signatures and Encryption*)[39] but it is closely linked and related to issues of Intellectual Property Rights protection as discussed below.

Copyright

The key question which the *Television Without Frontiers* Directive ignored was the potential restriction on Community-wide broadcasting posed by national copyright laws of the Member States.[40] The protection of copyright, and in particular the rights of authors, of performers, of film producers and broadcasters, lies at the heart of any market in film and television programmes. Therefore, the Community's aim was that the protection afforded to the intellectual property rights of film producers and broadcasters would be harmonized and extended throughout all Member States. The Community's work in this field began with the adoption, in 1988, of a Green Paper on copyright and the technological challenge,[41] but above all with the adoption, in 1990, of a working plan[42] in which the Commission defines a new approach incorporating the dual cultural and economic nature of copyright. This new approach emphasizes, in particular, that any harmonization of copyright and related rights must take place on the basis of an increased level of protection, owing to the fact that they are essen-

---

39. COM(97)503, 8 October 1997.
40. For an overview of the reasons and the problems see 'Film and Television in the Single European Market. Dreams and Delusions.' Inaugural Professional Lecture by Vincent Porter, 17 October 1991.
41. COM(88)172 final, 7.6.88.
42. *Following up the Green Paper, Commission working plan in the field of copyright and related rights*. COM(90)584 final, 17.1.91.

tial to cultural creativity and the fact that their protection makes it possible to guarantee maintenance and development of creativity in the interests of authors, the cultural industries, consumers and the community as a whole.

Five copyright directives, a Green Paper and consequent Directive proposal have so far emerged.[43] One of the first Directives relevant to the media was adopted by the Council in November 1992.[44] It provides exclusive rental rights and a non-transferable right of reasonable compensation in favour of the author, performing artists, phonogram and first film recording producers, along with some conditions of ownership. In October 1993 a Directive was published with the aim of harmonization of the term of protection of copyright.[45] A month later, the Council adopted the so-called 'Satellite and Cable Directive',[46] regulating the rebroadcasting of television programmes. It supplements the *Television Without Frontiers* Directive and aims to harmonize the legal framework of the single audio-visual area by, on the one hand, establishing the principle of the contractual acquisition of satellite communication rights in a single place and, on the other hand, that of collective management for the negotiation of cable retransmission rights. Finally, in 1996 a Directive providing copyright protection for computerized and manual databases was approved.[47] The Directive creates a new exclusive 'sui generis' right (which will last 15 years after completion) for database creators and harmonizes copyright law applicable to structures of databases. Along with the Green Paper on *Intellectual Property Rights in the Information Society*, (to be discussed in the following chapter)[48] the Directive is

---

43. For an overview see Schulze M., 'Developments in the field of European copyright law: The Magill and SACEM Judgments, Contents and Application of the Various Directives in the Field of Copyright Law' in *IRIS 1995: Legal Developments in the Audio-visual Sector*, p. 23.

44. Council Directive of 19 November 1992 on rental and lending rights related to coypright in the field of intellectual property. OJEC No L 346, 27 November 1992. Council Directive of 14 May 1991 on the legal protection of computer programmes, OJEC No L 122/42, 17 May 1991 was the first copyright directive.

45. Council Directive of 29 October 1993 harmonizing the term of protection of copyright and certain related rights. OJEC No L 290, 24 November 1993.

46. Council Directive of 27 September 1993 on the coordination of certain rules concerning copyright and rights related to copyright applicable to satellite broadcasting and cable re-transmission, OJEC No L 248, of 6 October 1993 .

47. Directive 96/9/EC of 11 March 1996 concerning the legal protection of databases. OJEC No L77:20.

48. COM (95)382, 19 July 1995.

particularly important for the creation of new communications services. Extensive consultations based on this Green Paper and international developments in this area[49] led in December 1997 to a Commission proposal for a Directive harmonizing aspects of rules on copyright and related rights in the Information Society.[50] The proposal would adjust and complement the existing legal framework, with particular emphasis on new products and services containing intellectual property (both on-line and on physical carriers such as CDs, CD-ROMs and Digital Video Discs), so as to ensure a single market in copyright and related rights while protecting and stimulating creativity and innovation within the European Union. It would in particular harmonize rules on the right of reproduction, the communication to the public right (including making protected material available on-demand over the Internet), the distribution right and the legal protection of anti-copying systems and information for managing rights. Meanwhile, the CJEC ruled in its famous *Magill* decision,[51] that abuse of a dominant position – in this case restricting competition[52] – should clearly be regarded as overstepping what is really necessary for the core functioning of copyright.[53]

Competition policy and media ownership

The emergence of large media companies and increased economic pressures have led to a situation of media concentrations and cross-ownership.[54] A certain degree of strength through size may well be desirable in some respects, but there is also a danger that

[49.] In particular, the proposal would implement the main obligations of new Treaties agreed in December 1996 in the framework of the World Intellectual Property Organization (WIPO) on the protection of authors and the protection of performers and phonogram producers.

[50.] See <http://europa.eu.int/comm/dg15/en/intprop/intprop/1100.htm>

[51.] *Radio Telefis Eireann (RTE) and Independent Television v the Commission,* C-241/91 P and C-242/91 P, 6 April 1995, [1995] AllER (EC) 416.

[52.] The ECJ ruled that RTE and Independent Television had abused dominant positions in not allowing Magill magazine to publish full listings of television programmes.

[53.] See, McGonagle M., *op. cit.* pp. 279–281.

[54.] For a detailed description See, Sanchez-Taberno A., *Media Concentration in Europe: Commercial Enterprise and the Public Interest* (The European Institute for the Media, 1993), Media Monograph No. 16.

further vertical and horizontal integration will force out competitors and lead to a lack of media pluralism. The devices used so far in the European Community to try to counteract these developments are the rules applying to undertakings under general EC competition policy.[55] Articles 85, 86 and 90 of the EC Treaty provided a basis for Member States to take action to eliminate anticompetitive behaviour. Article 85 is concerned with agreements that prevent, restrict or distort competition, while art. 86 prohibits abuse of a dominant position in the market. Nevertheless, under certain very specific conditions, the Treaty makes provision for an exception to this principle of prohibition by authorizing certain agreements between undertakings.[56] Both Articles are applied to the public sector (subject to certain exceptions) by art. 90. Since the Mergers Regulation (1989)[57] DGIV has also powers to vet (and to block) mergers with which comply with conditions as to size of turnover, both globally and within the European Union. A few cases can be used to illustrate the Commission's desire to monitor strict application of the rules of competition while taking account, particularly, of their effects on pluralism. Thus for example in the *MSG Media Service* case[58] the Commission prohibited the setting-up of a joint venture between major groups including Bertelsmann and Deutsche Bundespost Telekom, on the basis that such a joint venture would have the result of cutting off access to the German pay-TV market and thus limit access to the market for rival suppliers. In the case of *Nordic Satellite Distribution*[59] a similar result occurred. Finally, in the case of the *Holland Media Group* the Commission required the parties (in particular RTL4 and RTL5, as well as the VERONICA channel) to seek appropriate measures to guarantee that the Dutch market would remain open to rival

---

55. For a discussion on the role of competition policy in the regulation of (new) media concentrations see Prosser T., Goldberg D. and Verhulst S., *The Impact of New Communications Technologies on Media Concentrations and Pluralism.* (Council of Europe, MM-CM (96) 3), 1997, pp. 60–6.

56. Article 85(3) of the Treaty makes provision for an exemption to be granted in the case of agreements which fulfil the following four conditions: if they contribute to improving production or distribution; if they promote technical or economic progress; if they allow consumers a fair share of the resulting benefit; if they do not impose restrictions which are not indispensable to the attainment of the objectives of the agreement.

57. Council Regulation 4064/89/EEC on the control of concentrations between undertakings, OJ 1990 L 257/14.

58. Case Nr IV/M.469 *MSG Media Service*, 9 November 1994.

59. Case Nr IV/M.490 *Nordic Satellite Distribution*, 19 July 1995.

suppliers.[60] In general, the Commission deals with (broadly) two kinds of cases. First, cases concerning the restructuring of market positions, notably through the creation of transnational ventures, commonly referred to as 'strategic alliances', between media companies as they move into global markets. These are generally of a horizontal nature. A second group of cases concerns issues of convergence, particularly in the overlap of telecommunications and media: these cases tend to include strong vertical elements such as in the *MSG* case.[61]

However, since the late 1980s concerns have been expressed within the Community that competition policy fails to control media concentrations due to problems of market definition and issues of pluralism. Thus given the complexity of modern media markets, it is difficult to measure dominance by concentrating on the share of a single market such as television. Moreover, the normal economic concerns of competition law are complicated by a need to protect pluralism on political and social grounds. Even DG IV, responsible for competition policy, identified the media sector as one which may require specific legislation.[62] At the end of 1992 the European Commission published a Green Paper[63] which analysed the issue of concentration in the media and the need for action, and suggested possible courses of action. Option one was that no specific action should be taken at Community level; option two proposed co-operative action to ensure greater transparency of media ownership and control, whilst option three proposed to eliminate differences and to achieve harmonization between national restrictions on media ownership.[64] The Green Paper launched a wide consultation process, which culminated in the 1994

---

60. Case Nr IV/M.553 *Holland Media Group* (HMG), 20 September 1995.
61. See Ungerer H., *EU Competition Law in the Telecommunications, Media and Information Technology Sectors.* Fordham Corporate Law Institute – 22nd Annual Conference on International Antitrust Law & Policy – Fordham University, School of Law, New York City 27/10/1995, available at <http://europa.eu.int/en/comm/dg04/public/en/index.htm>
62. See Harcourt A.J., 'Regulating for Media Concentration: the Emerging Policy of the European Union' in: *Utilities Law Review*, Vol. 7, October 1996, pp. 202–10.
63. *Green Paper, Pluralism and Media Concentration in the Internal Market: An Assessment of the Need for Community Action*, COM(92)480 final, 23 December 1992.
64. For an overview of the responses see, Hitchens L.P., 'Media Ownership and Control: A European Approach', *The Modern Law Review*, 1994, Vol. 57, pp. 585–601.

follow up Commission Communication.[65] Since then, DGXV has produced several draft proposals for a Directive[66] but none has yet been approved by the Commission. DGXV is continuing to work on these draft proposals and the substance of any forthcoming Directive is still a matter for speculation.[67]

A second major concern of competition policy relates to the rules applying to Member States and particularly to aids granted by the States which are regarded as incompatible with the common market (Arts 92 *et. seq.* of the Treaty). The Member States promote the development of their audio-visual industries in various ways, particularly through direct grants for specific film productions, tax incentives for investment in companies in this sector, funding of training and support for film festivals. Such measures are generally consistent, as regards their objectives, with the Community's own audio-visual policy, which seeks, *inter alia*, to promote the competitiveness of the European programmes industry. Support measures may be local, regional or national. Insofar as they do not distort competition or affect trade between Member States to any significant extent, art. 92 does not apply and the Commission has no cause to intervene. However, as economic players on the relevant market frequently find themselves in competition, certain aid measures for the film and television production sectors may have an appreciable effect on competition and trade between Member States. The promotion of cultural diversity has already been accepted by the Commission as a justification for state aid to the film industry and the production of television programmes, provided the aid did not cause undue distortion of competition. The Treaty on European Union in art. 3(p) provides that 'The Community shall contribute to the flowering of the cultures of the Member States', and new Arts 92(3)(d) and 128 were inserted to implement this principle. However, this did not necessarily imply a fundamental shift in policy. Article 92(3)(d) provides that aid to promote culture and heritage conservation, where such

---

65. *Follow up of the Green Paper Pluralism and Media Concentration in the Internal Market: An Assessment of the Need for Community Action*, COM(94)353 final, October 1994.
66. See Beltrane F., 'Harmonising Media Ownership Rules: Problems and Prospects', in *Utilities Law Review*, Vol. 7, October 1996, pp. 172–5.
67. See Doyle G., 'From "Pluralism" to "Ownership": Europe's emergent policy on media concentrations navigates the doldrums' 1997 (3) *The Journal of Information, Law and Technology (JILT)* <http://elj.warwick.ac.uk/jilt/commsreg/97_3doyl/>

aid does not affect trading conditions and competition in the Community to an extent that is contrary to the common interest, may be regarded as compatible with the common market. The Commission had already taken such considerations into account when assessing aid in this sector. In its future assessment of state aid to the audio-visual sector, the Commission will continue to seek a balance between the requirements of cultural and heritage promotion, the openness of trade and competition in the single market and the need to avoid undue distortions. For an overview of proposed measures in the field of culture see *First Report On The Consideration Of Cultural Aspects In European Community Action* (European Commission 1994).

The funding of public service broadcasters has, of course, a special importance in this context. Under the rules governing state aid, the specific question of the funding of public service broadcasters has been raised with the Commission by private broadcasters from France, Spain and Portugal. The complaints are that public funding of public broadcasters through consumer levies, direct subsidies or periodic capital injections confers unfair advantages. The issue is of great importance and interest throughout the Community, and in the Amsterdam Treaty a Protocol was agreed to the effect that the provisions of the Treaty are without prejudice to the competence of Member States to fund public service broadcasting insofar as this does not affect competition in the Community to an extent contrary to the common interest.[68] This hardly resolves the problem, as it leaves unresolved the basic question of the extent to which the public interest can justify anti-competitive conduct and funding.

A final competition issue which is likely to be of very considerable importance in the future is that of conditional access (mentioned above). This refers to systems which allow individual subscribers access to services such as pay-television as well as being closely related to subscription management systems and electronic programme guides. The danger is that if the systems or technology owned by one enterprise obtain a dominant position this will restrict competition through giving the owner power over the 'gateways' to such access; it is highly improbable that consumers will buy more than one system. As regards digital television, the Community took action relatively early through the Advanced

---

[68.] *Treaty of Amsterdam Amending the Treaty on European Union* (1997), Protocol on the System of Public Service Broadcasting in the Member States; see p. 19 above.

Television Standards Directive mentioned above.[69] This requires Member States to take all necessary measures to ensure that operators of conditional access services offer services to all broadcasters on a fair, reasonable and non-discriminatory basis and to comply with Community competition law. Licensing of industrial property rights in conditional access technology is also to be carried out on fair, reasonable and non-discriminatory terms. The Directive has been implemented in the UK by the Advanced Television Standards Regulations,[70] but similar action has not been taken in some other Member States and its is likely that a considerable number of disputes will arise in the context of the imminent growth of digital television throughout Europe.

Commercial communications

Commercial communications, i.e. advertising, direct marketing, public relations and sales promotions play an essential role given the reliance by most audio-visual and other media on income generated by these activities for their existence. As described above, television advertising is mainly regulated by the *Television Without Frontiers* Directive and the Court of Justice has already dealt with some infringements of the advertising rules of the Directive. The TV Directive is however supplemented by the Council Directive 84/450/EEC of 10 September 1984[71] on the approximation of the laws, regulations and administrative provisions of the Member States concerning misleading advertising.[72] The latter was amended by the European Parliament and Council Directive 97/55/EC of 6 October 1997 so as to include comparative advertising.[72] In order to control misleading advertising, the Member States must ensure that those persons or organizations with a legitimate interest may bring a court action against misleading advertising and/or bring the advertising before a competent administrative body to rule on the complaints or to institute the appropriate legal proceedings. The Directive does however, not exclude voluntary control of misleading advertising by self-regula-

---

[69.] Directive 95/47/EC, OJ No 281:51–54, 23 November 1995.
[70.] SI 1996/3151.   [71.] OJ 1994 L 250.
[72.] Council Directive of 10 September 1984 concerning misleading and comparative advertising, OJ 1997 L 290.

tory bodies if such means of redress are provided for in addition to the court or administrative proceedings. The 1997 Directive introduces the concept of comparative advertising, which is defined as 'any advertising which explicitly or by implication identifies a competitor or goods or services offered by a competitor' and applies the provisions for controlling misleading advertising to this.

A Commission proposal for a directive on tobacco advertising, first put forward in 1989, has been discussed on ten occasions by the Health Council without reaching a common position. Under the Luxembourg Presidency, however, a compromise text was developed on the basis of the Commission's proposal, which can be summarized as follows:

- it regulates direct and indirect advertising, and sponsorship promoting tobacco products;
- it provides that no new tobacco products can bear the trademark of another product after the entry into force of the directive;
- it allows Member States to keep stronger national rules if they wish;
- it calls on the Commission to make regular reports on the application of the directive accompanied if necessary by proposals;
- it allows a period (unspecified) for transposition into national law and two years transition for phasing out indirect advertising and sponsorship. A further period may be allowed for existing sponsorship of events and activities organized at world level provided the sums devoted to such sponsorship decrease during the transitional period, and that voluntary agreements are put in place to reduce the impact of tobacco advertising at such events; and
- it permits tobacco trade publications, advertising at point-of-sale, presentation of tobacco products and their price, and import of third country publications containing tobacco advertising, to be subject to Member State regulation as they are excluded from the scope of the directive.[73]

Finally, the general future regulatory framework is set out in the Commission's Green Paper on Commercial Communications which will be relevant for transfrontier broadcasting and new in-

[73.] See MEMO/97/105, 1997-12-03.

formation services e.g. on-line services.[74] The Commission acknowledges in the Green Paper that national restrictions may be justifiable on public health and consumer protection grounds. It proposes a methodology to deliver a more uniform assessment of national measures, an *ad hoc* Committee to develop a more constructive dialogue between the Commission and the Member States, and a Commission information contact point which would be responsible for ensuring the effective collation and dissemination of information relating to the EU's policy in this field. A communication on an internal market framework for commercial communications based on home country control and mutual recognition is expected by the end of 1997. This Communication will be a follow-up to the consultations held in the framework of the Green Paper.

Conclusion

In this and the preceding chapter a bewildering range of activities, and indeed a bewildering range of themes, has been described ranging from measures to ensure freedom of transmission to measures affecting programme content and advertising time, and financial support for media industries to competition law. There have been some significant failures, notably the attempts to develop a European HDTV presence. However, the central core activity embodied in the *Television Without Frontiers* Directive has been relatively successful, and it is notable that the 1997 revision of the Directive did not seek to make significant inroads into its coverage but rather to clarify and extend it. Competition law has also had some influence, although as we shall see shortly it has been far more important in the area of telecommunications and attempts to develop new rules on media ownership have so far been unsuccessful.

Most of the discussion in this chapter has concerned the 'old' media and in particular broadcasting. They are currently being overtaken, however, by the process of convergence and the development of 'new' media leading to the so-called 'information society'. What activities has the Community carried out in relation to these developments? This will be the theme of our next chapter.

---

74. COM(96)192 final. See also <http://www.cec.lu/en/record/green/gp006/en/index.html>

CHAPTER SEVEN

The information society

Since 1994, all EC audio-visual (and telecommunications) related policies have been overshadowed by the concept of the 'information society'.[1] While other nations and authorities have talked of 'information super-highways', or 'national information infrastructures', the European Community prefers the phrase 'information society' since it 'reflects [more accurately] their awareness that there are very broad social and organizational changes which have to be confronted as a result of the information and communications revolution'.[2] The idea is not new and has been heralded before but it has received renewed attention under the influence of recent technological and market developments which lead towards the convergence of telecommunications, media and information technology.

As highlighted in many EC documents, it is considered as of paramount importance that new ways be found to increase the competitiveness of European industry relative to its international competitors thus allowing firms in Europe to obtain and sustain leadership positions in key information technology and multi-media sectors. This can be considered as the key driver behind most EC actions in this field, as it was in the case of audio-visual policy. It is however clear that the Commission considers that convergence will ultimately affect all aspects of life and that the overall framework should not be limited to the technological and economic dimension alone, but must focus on the whole spectrum of societal and cultural values, a dimension the Commission did

---

[1.] See Schoof H. and Watson Brown A., 'Information highways and media policies in the European Union' in: *Telecommunications Policy*, 1995, Vol. 19, No. 4, pp. 325–338.

[2.] See The Union's policies – Information Society, Telecommunications at <http://europa.eu.int/pol/infso/en/info.htm>

not acknowledge in the eighties when developing a broadband policy. Moreover different and separate policies were developed in the past for the media, for information technology and for the telecommunications sector. Convergence will however require a policy framework that encompasses all media and aims to be free from inconsistencies between policies in different sectors.[3]

The Bangemann Report and Action Plan

It was the *White Paper on Growth, Competitiveness and Employment*,[4] published in 1993, which first emphasized the significance of the information society for the future of Europe. It linked the creation of a common European information infrastructure to the creation of new markets and jobs and to European economic growth and competitiveness. Following the proposals, the Council asked for the establishment of a task force or high-level group of experts to present a report on the information society which would suggest concrete measures for its implementation. The group, chaired by Commissioner Martin Bangemann and consisting of representatives of government, industry and consumers, submitted its report to the European Council in Corfu in June 1994.[5] It highlighted the urgency of Community action to ensure that European enterprises remain competitive internationally, and highlighted the need to speed up the process of liberalization of the telecommunications sector and the need for new regulatory safeguards. The report also specified that financing information infrastructure should be left to the private sector, the task of the public sector being to assume an enabling and catalytic function. Therefore, a list of ten initiatives was proposed aimed at demonstrating the feasibility and usefulness of new telematic applications and a coherent statutory framework to avoid the circulation of information being impeded by different national regulations. Also important is the recognition in the report that the audio-visual media are crucial for stimulating

---

3. For a detailed overview of the policy issues related to this topic, see, *Public Policy Issues Arising from Telecommunications and Audio-visual Convergence. Report for the European Commission.* (KPMG, September 1996).
4. COM(93)700, 5 December 1993.
5. See Bangemann, M., *et al.*: *Europe and the global information society – Recommendations to the European Council, a report prepared for the European Council meeting 24–25 June 1994.*

the domestic multimedia market which might otherwise be resistant to the initial costs of the required equipment.[6]

The Bangemann Report was fully endorsed by the Council and the European Parliament. Consequently the Commission produced a Communication, *Europe's way to the information society. An Action Plan.*[7] It constituted a general framework within which actions in different fields relating to the information society must be structured and mutually consolidated. This plan of action was accompanied by a timetable covering 1994 and 1995. Four main lines of action were put forward:

- adaptation of a statutory and legal framework,[8] the central element of which was liberalization of infrastructure (see below). Important measures were also adopted and proposed relating to the definition of universal service and its financing, interconnection and interoperability through open network provision, intellectual property rights, electronic security, media control and the international dimension;

- encouragement of initiatives in the field of transeuropean networks, services, applications and content. In addition to the use of traditional instruments such as the funding of research and technological development programmes,[9] the Commission intended to act as a catalyst for initiatives from the private sector, the Member States, regions and cities, particularly through the 'Information Society Project Office' (ISPO)[10] whose role would be to encourage and facilitate the setting up of partnerships for launching applications;

- as regards social and cultural aspects of the information society, a High-level Group of senior experts was set up in May 1995 by the Commission to look into social and societal changes which accompany the continuing development towards an

---

6. *Ibid.*, pp. 9–10.   7. COM(94)347, 19 July 1994.
8. For a complete overview see *The Rolling Action Plan*, COM(96)607, at <http://www.ispo.cec.be/infosoc/legreg/rap2.doc>
9. The main funded programmes are: ACTS (Advanced Communications Technologies and Services), RACE (cf. *supra*), ESPRIT (cf. *supra*), Telematics Applications Programme, The INFO2000 Programme (Multimedia Content), Task Force Multimedia Educational Software and TEN-TELECOM '96 (Implementations of TransEuropean Networks) See, <http://www2.echo.lu/home.html>. Meanwhile the 5th RTD Framework has also been launched.
10. See <http://www.ispo.cec.be/>

information society. In its interim report[11] the group highlighted a number of aspects of the use of information and communication technologies and made more than hundred recommendations. Those were examined, together with the first report of the Information Society Forum[12] at the Council of Ministers' summit in Dublin in July 1996; and

■ promotion of the information society through activities (e.g. Information Society Awareness Week) to explain the issues of the Information Society, as perceived by the Commission.

New priorities

In the light of technological and other changes, and new issues arising, it became necessary in 1996 to reappraise the action plan and to propose new priorities. The main policy objectives in the field of the so-called information society were therefore updated and outlined in July 1996 by the European Commission Communication 'Europe at the Forefront of the Global Information Society: Rolling Action Plan'.[13] Four new priority areas and consequent initiatives were identified:[14]

11. *Building the European information superhighway for us all. First reflections of the High Level Group of Experts. Interim report.* Brussels: DGV, January 1996.
12. *Networks for People and their Communities. Making the Most of the Information Society in the European Union. First Annual Report to the European Commission from the Information Society Forum,* June 1996.
13. At the same time four new documents were submitted responding to some of these new political priorities: Communication COM(96)395 on *The Implications of Information Society on European Union Policies – Preparing the Next Steps* (this is of particular political importance as it lays the foundation for adapting the Action Plan which the Commission would carry out by the end of 1996 in order to take into account new strategic priorities); Green Paper COM(96)389 *Living and Working in the Information Society: People First,* 22 July 1996 (intended to deepen political, social and civil dialogue on the most important social and societal aspects of the information society); Communication COM(96)359 on *Standardisation and the Global Information Society* (examines how, in the light of the characteristics of the ICT market and the ICT standardization process, the best possible conditions can be created for the drawing up of the standards needed for the implementation of the information society); Draft Directive *Regulatory Transparency in the Internal Market for Information Society Services* (sets up an information mechanism on legislative initiatives of the Member States).
14. See also *New Priorities for The Information Society. Background Report –* BR/15/96, (European Commission Representation in the United Kingdom, December 1996), at: <http://www.cec.org.uk/pubs/br/br96/br9615.htm>

- improving the conditions for business;
- investing in the future by research and training;
- using information technology to benefit peoples' lives; and
- reducing the discrepancies between the developed and developing nations.

A brief discussion of these follows.

Firstly, improving the business environment was to be achieved through the efficient and coherent implementation of the liberalized telecommunications environment, the thorough application of internal market principles and promoting the introduction of new technologies into daily business activities. Full telecommunications liberalization has always been considered as crucial for the development and creation of the information society. However as telecommunications operates across borders, there is a growing need for increased cooperation between national authorities, especially in the areas of frequency allocation, licensing, numbering and relations with external bodies like the International Telecommunications Union. The Commission therefore considered whether an European Union level telecommunications regulatory body would be needed (see below). Moreover, the Commission also believed that fair competition and proper working of the internal market would require complete consistency between the national laws relating to information services. Inconsistent national legislation could create new barriers, hence the Commission's proposal discussed under regulatory transparency, below. Existing legislation in the European Union was to be examined for inconsistency in the light of the convergence of the technologies of telecommunications, electronic information services and broadcasting. Finally the Commission also prepared proposals to ensure confidentiality and electronic authentication so that wide business use of the new techniques would be protected and thus encouraged. The Commission believed especially that industrial success in Europe depended on the rapid uptake of information and communication technologies by business, and especially by SMEs which account for over two-thirds of the European workforce.

Secondly, the Florence Summit gave impetus to the educational dimension of the information society strategy by asking the Commission to adopt an initiative, 'Learning in the Information Society', to be implemented in an action plan covering interconnecting networks of schools, the promotion of the educational content of multimedia and the use of new training tools. However, adapting educational structures and the learning process remains mainly a responsibility of the Member States. It was concluded that research should be focused on addressing specific user needs, and that this approach would require an interdisciplinary approach. The Fifth Framework Programme for Research and Technological Development therefore, gave priority to research related to information technologies,[15] particularly in the development of technology, infrastructure, services, applications and content.

Thirdly, the Commission was to establish a number of actions to address the key issues relating to the implications of the information society for the citizen. At the same time, the process of using the advantages of the information society in the context of regional policy to promote European cohesion would be addressed. Another important element in this context was the protection of fundamental rights and freedoms, such as the right to privacy, in the information society (see the discussion of data protection and the media below). Moreover, information technology should be used increasingly to improve the efficiency and openness of public services. The Commission intended to encourage the uptake of electronic communication techniques by national administrations and in its own operations.

Finally, while the initial Action Plan did not fully reflect the importance of global cooperation, it became clear to the European Commission that setting global rules is an essential element of the information society. Global rules concern market access, intellectual property rights, privacy and data protection, harmful and illegal on-line content, tax issues, information security, frequencies, interoperability and standards. In this context, Commissioner Bangemann launched a call in 1997 to governments, regulators and industry to work together to establish a new global framework for communications for the next millennium during speeches in Geneva[16] and Venice.[17]

---

15. See COM(96)332, p.7.
16. See <http://www.ispo.cec.be/infosoc/promo/speech/geneva.html>
17. See <http://www.ispo.cec.be/infosoc/promo/speech/venice.html>

International conferences

The organization of, and participation in, international conferences has been a major policy-instrument of the European Union in the field of the information society. At least three conferences are regarded as landmarks in the development of the EUs vision.

The Conference at G7 ministerial level on information society, held in Brussels on 25–6 February 1995 was the first. The meeting emphasized the necessity of encouraging the development of a worldwide information society. Eleven pilot projects were identified for international cooperation. The implementation of the G7 conclusions across the different EC policies related to the information society is currently under way and a progress report on the pilot project was presented at the Halifax G7 meeting in June 1997. The South African Vice President proposed at the Brussels G7 Conference an Information Society Conference with the developing countries hosted by South Africa. The International Conference on Information Society and Development (ISAD) took place in South Africa during May 1996 with the participation of many developing countries. Contacts have been established with the Egyptian government for the preparation of a follow-up meeting. A Communication on 'The Information Society and Development: the Role of the European Union'[18] was published in July 1997 as a follow-up to the ISAD Conference. It focuses on the redefinition and the re-orientation of previous policies to give a higher priority in development policies to telecommunications infrastructures and applications.

Finally, at the beginning of July 1997 an International Conference at ministerial level on 'Global information networks' was held in Bonn. At this international ministerial conference, ministers from 29 European countries agreed on a number of key principles that would pave the way for a rapid growth in Europe of the use of global information networks. Representatives of leading European businesses and of European user groups attending the Conference supported in separate statements this drive to stimulate the use of the information networks in Europe and beyond. The ministers undertook to develop further their national strategies and action plans and to strengthen their cooperation at the European and international level.[19]

18. COM(97)351.
19. Information on the Bonn Conference is available on <http://www2.echo.lu/bonn/.>

Regulatory transparency

Within the framework described above, there are more than 400 accomplished, pending, on-going and forthcoming actions. In order to coordinate all those actions and the actions taken by its Member States, the Communication and the accompanying proposal for a Council Directive concerning regulatory transparency in the internal market for information society services[20] addresses the concern that the regulatory activity for which the ground is being prepared in the Member States might, if it is not monitored, jeopardise attainment of the Internal Market objective.[21] The Communication states: 'Because of all the new developing products and services, many Member States have been preparing new legislation to regulate them. If these initiatives were left uncoordinated, it is very likely that new market distortions would arise'. Re-fragmentation and overregulation are also cited as possible consequences of the lack of transparency.[22] Moreover, 'these services might give rise to different risks from those covered by the existing rules and regulations on traditional services or on television broadcasting or telecommunication services'. The Commission has therefore proposed to bring information services[23] within the scope of the existing Directive 83/189/EEC laying down a procedure for the provision of information in the fields of technical standards and regulations[24] and to develop a 'transparency mechanism'. The latter should alert the Community to any inconsistencies with other national or Community laws, or any potential trade barriers arising from a new proposal. It reproduces the procedural measures laid down in Directive 83/189/EEC, which are as follows:

20. COM(96)392 final, 30 August 1996.   21. *Ibid.*, p. 23.

22. 'that is to say, of the introduction of new, unjustified or excessive obstacles to the free movement of services between Member States and to the freedom of establishment for the providers of such services, which might, moreover, have repercussions at Community level in the form of overregulation or mutually inconsistent regulations.'

23. Under 'information services', the proposal includes: on-line professional services, e.g. those of solicitors, stockbrokers, health services; interactive entertainment services, e.g. video on demand, on-line video games; on-line information services, e.g. electronic libraries, on-line weather forecasting, on-line financial information, virtual shopping malls, on-line electronic newspapers, on-line tourism services, on-line estate agents, on-line insurance services, and on-line educational services. It will not cover television or radio broadcasting, teletext, mail order, automatic bank tellers, electronic games of the amusement arcade type, or voice telephony services.

24. OJ 1983 L 109.

- a procedure for the provision of information on draft rules and regulations on information services: the Member States would have to communicate to the Commission any draft provision which will be applicable to information society services. The Commission will forward the information to all the other Member States in order to make them aware of national initiatives;

- a consultation procedure: following notification of the draft rule or regulation, an initial standstill period of three months starts to run during which the Member States and the Commission may make comments or deliver a detailed opinion (in which case the total standstill period is extended to six months), or, in the case of the Commission, declare that a future harmonization proposal will be presented or that it has already proposed harmonization measures in the field concerned (in which case the total standstill period is extended to 12 months and may be as long as 18 months);

- a committee: the committee of Member States' representatives already provided for in Directive 83/189/EEC will enable the authorities to stimulate a dialogue between Member States' legislators and promote administrative cooperation. At a time when in many Member States talks on the legal framework for services are already under way, the committee might constitute a particularly useful forum in which the authorities can meet and express their views.

Finally, political agreement was reached on a common position concerning a Directive based on the earlier proposals on 27 November 1997.[25]

The information society and telecommunications policy[26]

The view of the EC has always been that the development of an information society crucially depends upon an efficient and highly

---

25. See *Press Release IP/97/1054*, 28 November 1997.
26. For a comprehensive and detailed description see *Status Report On European Union Telecommunications Policy*, Brussels, 7 May 1997, DGXIII/A/1 and for a good general account Hunt, A., 'Regulation of Telecommunications: the Developing EU Regulatory Framework and its Impact on the United Kingdom', (1997) 3 *European Public Law*, 93–115.

developed telecommunications network being in place, capable of carrying the full range of information society applications. In order to achieve that vision, a package of measures was required to open up the European market to competition and to provide the regulatory safeguards necessary to attract and sustain new entrants while protecting the interests of consumers and users. The Commission proposed a package of measures which includes the liberalization of telecommunications infrastructure and services, the implementation of Open Network Provision measures and the establishment of universal service rules. A brief discussion follows.

In the 1987 Green Paper on the development of the common market for telecommunications services and equipment,[27] the Commission proposed the introduction of more competition in the telecommunications market combined with a greater degree of harmonization in order to enjoy to a maximum extent the opportunities offered by a single EC market, in particular in terms of economies of scale. The Green Paper proposals received broad general support from market participants and the Commission prepared a programme of action which was supported by Council[28] and the European Parliament, as well as by the Economic and Social Committee. This programme included the following actions:

- rapid full opening of the terminal equipment market to competition (section III.A.1);
- full mutual recognition of type-approval for terminal equipment (section III.H);
- progressive opening of telecommunications markets to competition (section III.A);
- clear separation of regulatory and operational activities in the Member States to conform with the EC Treaty competition rules (section III.A.2);
- establishment of open access conditions to networks and services through the Open Network Provision (ONP) programme (section III.B);
- establishment of the European Telecommunications Standards

---

27. *Towards a dynamic European economy: Green Paper on the development of the common market for telecommunications services and equipment*, COM(87)290 final, 30.06.1987.
28. Council Resolution of 30 June 1988 on the development of the common market for telecommunications services and equipment up to 1992 (88/C 257/01; OJ 1988 C 257/1).

Institute (ETSI), in order to stimulate European standardization (this was implemented in 1988); and
- full application of Community competition rules to the sector (section II.C).

These actions have subsequently been implemented to a large extent through the adoption of a series of legislative measures. The common theme of the policy mix which has emerged is the evolving balance to be struck between liberalization and harmonization, competition and public service. This balance has resulted from the commonly called 1989 'compromise' reached between the EC institutions, and was firstly reflected by the joint adoption in 1990 of two Directives introducing competition in the telecommunications services market (notably for value-added services and data networks)[29] and establishing a framework for harmonization at Community level[30] (see sections III.A.2 and III.B.1). In terms of practical results, the most important is that Member States fully liberalize public voice telephony by 1 January 1998, and this was implemented on time.[31]

The issue of interconnection is considered crucial for the development of the information society. In 1995 the Commission presented a proposal[32] applying the Open Network Principles (see below) to interconnection and interoperability. This proposal aimed to ensure open access to networks and services, and to guarantee the rights of new market entrants to obtain interconnection with infrastructure belonging to other operators. The Draft Communication on the application of the competition rules to access agreements in the telecommunications sector,[33] published in December 1996, aimed to clarify the role competition rules would play in resolving access agreements in the telecoms sector. It did not establish new principles of competition law, but demonstrated how the principles existing in current case law of the Commission and of the Court of Justice would be applied to a new type of

---

[29.] Commission Directive of 16 May 1988 on competition in the markets in telecommunications equipment (88/301/EEC; OJ 1988 L131/73).

[30.] Council Directive of 28 June 1990 on the establishment of the internal market for telecommunications services through the implementation of open network provision (90/387/EEC; OJ 1990 L192/1).

[31.] Directive 96/16/EC, OJ 1996 L74/13; Luxembourg, Greece, Spain, Portugal and Ireland may benefit from derogation for a limited period.

[32.] OJ 1995 C 237.   [33.] COM(96)649, OJ: C76.

problem occurring in the context of the liberalization of the telecoms sector. It set out access principles stemming from EU competition law, defined and clarified the relationship between competition law and sector-specific legislation and explained how competition rules will be applied in a consistent way across the converging sectors involved in the provision of new multimedia services, especially to access issues and gateways.

Perhaps even more important was the Council decision on the Multilateral Negotiations on basic telecommunications services in the context of the World Trade Organization (WTO), adopted 15 July 1997. The agreement, to enter force on 1 January 1998, was signed by 69 countries on 15 February 1997. It committed all signatories to important measures, in particular most-favoured nation (MFN) treatment banning discriminatory measures on a bilateral basis, as well as legally binding commitments regarding market access and national treatment. In addition, 54 countries agreed on a common set of regulatory principles aimed at securing more effective access and national treatment, in particular transparency, fairness and non-discrimination, in key areas such as interconnection, licensing, tariffs, universal service provisions, technical standards and frequencies. This also included a ban on anti-competitive practices such as cross-subsidy and disguised barriers to market access. The Commission negotiated on behalf of the Community and its Member States.

The initial Community reforms in the telecom sector only involved the liberalization of services, not infrastructure. However, the Community admitted that service liberalization alone would not be sufficient to attract new entrants and stimulate competition. Therefore, it adopted parallel 'harmonization' measures to ensure open and efficient access to networks and services. The concept of Open Network Provision (ONP) was first presented in a Green Paper in 1987.[34] In 1990 the Community adopted an ONP Framework Directive[35] which established general principles relating to the provision and use of networks and services, tariff principles and technical interfaces of network connections. This was followed by a series of measures implementing ONP. In December 1995 the Directive on the application of ONP to voice telephony was adopted.[36] Its three fundamental objectives were:

34. COM(87)290, June 1987.
35. Directive 90/387/EEC, OJ 1990 L 192.
36. Directive 95/62/EC, OJ 1995 L 321/6.

- determining the rights of the users of voice telephony services in their relations with telecommunications bodies;
- improving access for all users, including the providers of services, to the fixed infrastructure of public telephone networks (the Directive does not apply to mobile telephones); and
- encouraging the provision of voice telephony services at Community level.

Finally, it is generally accepted at a European level that in a liberalized telecommunications market, all citizens should be able to access a minimum level of service at an affordable cost. This principle of universal service was set out in the Communication on Universal Service in Telecommunications adopted in March 1996.[37] Building on the consensus established around the infrastructure Green Paper, the Commission presented a survey of the level and availability of universal service within the EU. It drew together the elements of the 1998 package relating to universal service to propose a strengthening of the concept for voice telephony services, in particular with regard to affordability and quality of service, and also examined the impact of universal service on regional and social cohesion, criteria for its evolution over time and the relationship between universal service and the information society. This was followed in November 1996 by a Communication on the assessment criteria for national schemes for the costing and financing of universal service and guidelines for the Member States on the operation of such schemes.[38] In order to assist Member States in preparing national reforms in advance of full liberalization of telecoms in 1998, this Communication identified the principal elements that the Commission would assess in looking at national universal service schemes which had to be notified to the Commission by the end of 1996. It also provide detailed guidelines, building on the existing principles within Community law, designed to develop best practice in national approaches to the costing and financing of universal service.

The Directive on interconnection in the context of ONP and universal service, published in June 1997 provides, not only a common framework for interconnection between the organizations operating public telecommunications networks in order to ensure 'any-to-any' services throughout the Community, but it also sets

37. COM(96)73.   38. COM(96)608.

principles for the costing and financing of universal service. Finally the Directive on the application of ONP to voice telephony and on universal service for telecommunications in a competitive environment revises and replaces the existing Directive on the application of ONP to voice telephony (see above). It describes the scope of universal service for telecommunications which must be available to all users in the EU and requires Member States to ensure that this service is affordable, taking into account national situations. The Directive also sets out harmonized conditions for the provision of fixed public telephone networks and publicly available telephone services in the EU.

Funding programmes

The European Union has developed within the context of the newer communications services numerous funding and research programmes. The overall objective of those programmes is to contribute to the healthy growth of the information infrastructure so that European industry can achieve greater competitiveness. A non-exhaustive overview of the main programmes follows:

- The ACTS Programme (Advanced Communications Technologies and Services) represents the European Commission's major effort to support precompetitive RTD (Research and Technological Development) in the context of trials in the field of telecommunications during the period of the Fourth Framework Programme of scientific research and development (1994–98);
- RACE was a collaborative European research programme, running from June 1987 to December 1995 (including Phases I & II and extension). It received a financial contribution from the European Community of 1103 million ECU. The overall objective was the introduction of Integrated Broadband Communication (IBC) taking into account evolving ISDN and national introduction strategies, progressing towards Community-wide services by 1995;
- ESPRIT is an initiative of the European Commission DGIII (Industry). The technological areas to be supported include software technologies, multimedia systems and high performance computing and networking;

- The Telematics application programme covers research, technological development and demonstration projects for telematics applications and support actions in thirteen sectors of the programme, including administration, transport, research, education and training, urban and rural areas and the environment;
- INFO2000 is a programme aiming to stimulate the European multimedia content industry and to encourage the use of multimedia content in the information society. Its action lines address, among others, legal issues, new multimedia projects, geographic information, market studies, standardization and skills development;
- Multilingual Information Society (MLIS) is a programme promoting the linguistic diversity of the EU in the information society. It is intended to raise awareness of, and stimulate provision of, multilingual services, favourable conditions for the language industries, reduced cost of information transfer among languages, and contribute to the promotion of linguistic diversity;
- Trans-European Telecommunications Networks (TEN-TELECOM) is a programme to promote the implementation of trans-European services and applications of the information society, based on the use of telecommunication infrastructures. It focuses on projects demonstrating clear socio-economic benefits and sufficiently mature to be deployed in the short term, and where a financial commitment by public and private parties depends upon an initial aid, at Union level;
- Finally, the 5th Framework Programme (1998–2002) concentrates on a limited number of topics and creates strong links between research and the needs of citizens and industry. It also calls for greater coordination both within the programme and with Member State research as well as greater managerial flexibility. The proposal identifies three thematic programmes (the living world and the ecosystem; a user-friendly information society; competitive and sustainable growth) and three horizontal programmes (the international dimension; research, innovation and SMEs; the human potential).

Social aspects of the information society

The High Level Expert Group (HLEG) on the social and societal aspects of the information society was established by the European Commission in May 1995, to examine how information and communications technologies are likely to affect the life chances and lifestyles of the Europeans. It published its Final Report *Building the European Information Society for us all* in April 1997.[39] This focuses on the following themes: employment and job creation; social and democratic values; culture and the future of new services and the media; universal access and consumer protection and support; sustainability in an information society; public services: bringing administration closer to citizens; and lifelong learning.

In general, the Group, which is composed of 14 renowned independent experts, argued in favour of a European model of the information society. This ought to be characterized by a strong ethos of solidarity, and should include all aspects of a broader social (not just industrial and economic) view of technological change. The Group considered that there was an urgent need to coordinate policies aimed at enhancing the job growth potential of the Information Society, and to make rapid progress towards establishing common minimum European social standards as part of creating a level playing field in the social sphere.

Building on an Interim Report presented in January 1996, the final report analysed a broad set of issues facing policy makers as Europe moves towards the full development of an information society. Some of the key conclusions of the report were as follows:[40]

- a mixed picture was apparent as regards the employment implications of the information society. There were certainly major opportunities for the growth of totally new forms of employment in it. The challenge was to identify how to make these new sectors develop rapidly in order to create jobs for the future;
- it was essential to view the information society as a 'learning society' based on the know-how and wisdom of people, not on information in machines, and so it was necessary to invest in human resources. One of the main challenges was to develop the skills to make effective use of information. The acquisition

---

[39] CE-05-97-907-EN-C.   [40] See <http://www.ispo.cec.be/hleg/hleg.html>

of these skills would be a lifelong learning process starting from formal school age and taking place both at work and at home;

■ new forms of work organization were emerging in the information society. The need for workers to be in the same place at the same time has been reduced by new technologies. These were potentially great advantages, but it was also necessary to exercise caution and find ways to ensure that workers were adequately protected;

■ it was essential to ensure that social cohesion issues are taken into account, and avoid the creation of new groups of excluded people in the drive towards the information society. In particular, people and communities must be given support in adapting to the information society, and the way these technologies are applied must be adapted to the needs of people; and

■ a fundamental rethinking of regional cohesion policies was called for. More effective instruments were needed to support demand-led regional policies for those areas/regions with a development shortfall where the potential benefits of technology were unlikely to filter through.

The Information Society Forum (another advisory group) is composed of around 130 members from six main fields: users of new technologies, social groups, content and services providers, network operators, equipment manufacturers and institutions. The Forum used similar arguments to the HLEG in its first annual report of June 1996.[41]

There are also other advisory groups of considerable importance in this area. Thus, replacing the Group of Advisers on the Ethical Implications of Biotechnology set up in 1991, the European Group on Ethics in Science and New Technologies was set up at the end of 1997.[42] Its mandate is wider than the previous body, covering not merely the ethical implications of developments in biotechnology, but science in general and new technologies. It is composed of 12 persons, including the nine from the previous Group; each serves for three years, is entirely independent from the Commission, and from national political and economic interests.

---

41. *Network for People and their Communities: Making the Most of the Information Society in the European Union,* at: <http://www.ispo.cec.be/infoforum/pub/fap/contents.htm>
42. IP/97/1196 Brussels, 31 December 1997.

The Commission will invite the Group to give its opinion on specific matters, but it is also free to investigate proactively; the Group is expected to work closely with other EU institutions.

A High-level Think Tank on Future Audiovisual Policy of the European Union was established on November 3 1997 to 'reflect on future audio-visual policy guidelines for the European Union'.[43] In particular, the Think Tank will reflect on the shortcomings, problems and challenges posed by the imminent digital technology revolution which the Commission believes is 'set to transform the European audio-visual landscape'. Four underlying principles are to be considered:

- new information and communication technologies must be incorporated into the process of European programme-making and marketing;
- the European audio-visual industry must improve its competitiveness and establish a worldwide presence;
- cultural diversity and the potential for society of the audio-visual industry must be given a higher profile; and
- full account must be taken of the general interest and the European approach in designing and implementing Community financial and legal instruments for the audiovisual sector.

The Think Tank is to address several specific questions:

- how can the European content production industry (film, television, multimedia) get the most out of these developments;
- how can the authorities at European and national level rise to the industrial, cultural and societal challenges; and
- what consideration is to be given to the general interest, in particular ethical considerations, in the new audio-visual landscape in order to safeguard the European approach to society?

The inclusion of this last question would seem to imply some overlap between the mandate of this High-Level Think Tank and that of the European Group on Ethics in Science and New Technologies. Having analysed these questions, the Group is to make recommendations to the Commission in the form of a Report, which will be circulated to the European Parliament, Council of Ministers and national governments. The report is to be delivered in

---

43. IP/97/941 Brussels, 3 November 1997 and MEMO/97/92.

September 1998. The final objective is a new audio-visual policy by the year 2000.

The Convergence Green Paper

On the third of December 1997, a long awaited Green Paper on the convergence of the telecommunications, media and information technology (IT) sectors was finally published.[44] The Green Paper launched a Europe-wide debate on how this new generation of electronic media should be regulated in the next century. It avoids however pre-packaged answers, but asked open questions about the future, particularly about the extent and speed of change. One key message is that convergence should not lead to additional regulation. Current rules should be reviewed to check whether they will still be relevant in the light of convergence.

Moreover, the Green Paper argues that the development of new services could be hindered by the existence of a range of barriers, including regulatory barriers, at different levels of the market. There are, however, differing views on the adequacy of existing regulatory frameworks to deal with the changing environment. One view is that the development of new products and services is being held back by regulatory uncertainty – that existing rules were defined for a national, analogue and mono-media environment, but that services increasingly cut across different traditional sectors and geographical boundaries, and they may be provided over a variety of platforms. This calls into question the underlying rationale for regulatory approaches in the different sectors affected by convergence. Proponents of this view would argue that such regulatory uncertainty holds back investment and damages the prospects for the implementation of the information society. An alternative view would hold that the specific characteristics of the existing separate sectors will limit the scope for service convergence, and would contend that the role of the media industry as the bearer of social, cultural and ethical values within our society is independent of the technology relied upon to reach the consumer. This would mean that regulation of economic conditions

---

44. *Green Paper on the Convergence of Telecommunications, Media and Information Technologies*, Commission of the European Communities, COM(97)623 December 1997. Available at: <http://www.ispo.cec.be/convergencegp/97623.html>

and that of the provision of information services should be separated to ensure efficiency and quality. According to the Green Paper, these matters need to be debated and resolved. Finding solutions will need to take account of the full range of interests in the various sectors affected by convergence. At the same time, the potential for change will be felt in different ways and at different levels (e.g. technology, industry, services and markets). Whilst digitalization means that convergence is well advanced at the level of technology, the Green Paper does not automatically assume that convergence at one level inevitably leads to the same degree of convergence at other levels. Equally, there is no assumption that convergence in technologies, industries, services and/or markets will necessarily imply a need for a uniform regulatory environment.

The Green Paper was produced as a response to the requirement for debate. It is divided into five chapters and is consciously interrogative, analysing issues and options and posing questions for public comment. At this stage the Commission had not taken a position nor reached any conclusions. In Chapters I and II, the Green Paper analyses the multiple technological and market aspects of the convergence phenomenon and their possible impact on the telecommunication, media and information technology sectors. Chapter III identifies the actual and potential market, industrial and regulatory barriers which may impede these technological and market developments. Chapter IV provides a detailed discussion of existing and possible future regulatory frameworks or approaches on issues like definitions, market entry and licensing, access to networks, conditional access systems and content, access to frequency spectrum, standards, pricing and individual consumer interests together with the international dimension. Finally, Chapter V proposes a set of principles for the future regulatory policy in the sectors affected by convergence. As set out in the Green Paper, these are:

- *regulation should be limited to what is strictly necessary to achieve clearly identified objectives.* Given the speed, dynamism and power of innovation of the sectors impacted by convergence, public authorities must avoid approaches which lead to over-regulation, or which simply seek to extend existing rules in the telecommunications and media sectors to areas and activities which are largely unregulated today. Any rules put in place should be tailored to meet clearly identified objectives in a proportionate manner;

- *future regulatory approaches should respond to the needs of users.* A key priority of any regulatory framework should be to seek to meet the needs of users in terms of offering them more choice, improving levels of service and lower prices, whilst fully guaranteeing consumer rights and the general public interest. Such an approach is fully consistent with wider policy goals which recognize the important role of many of the sectors in bringing the information society into citizens' everyday lives;
- *regulatory decisions should be guided by a need for a clear and predictable framework.* Regulators should seek to ensure a clear and predictable framework within which business can invest. Where issues can be left to market players, this should be made clear. Where new activities create uncertainty as to how and if they should be regulated, this should be clarified. This does not mean that the framework may not evolve, but it should do so against predetermined criteria, maintaining as far as possible the flexibility to respond to changes in a fast-moving market;
- *ensuring full participation in a converged environment.* Building on existing concepts of universal service in telecommunications and the public service mission in broadcasting, public authorities should seek to ensure that everyone is able to participate in the information society. Convergence in this context is likely to offer new means of participation; and
- *independent and effective regulators will be central to a converging environment.* Whilst the general trend is towards lighter regulation, the increased competition brought on by convergence underlines the need for effective and independent regulators. Regulatory independence is particularly important where the state retains a shareholding in any market player.

The Commission believes that the five month public consultation and public hearing period following the Green Paper will allow broad participation and debate of issues which are important for citizens, business and the further development of the information society. The Commission intends to produce a Communication by June 1998 based on the comments to be received from all interested parties within the consultation period. This June Communication, setting out the results of the public consultation, will allow political positions to be taken by the European Parliament, the Council of Ministers, the Economic and Social Committee and the Committee of the Regions, and for clear objectives for future policy to be established.

According to the Commission, the Green Paper initiates a new phase in the European Union's policy approach to the communications environment. As such it represents a key element of the overall framework put in place to support the development of an information society. It builds on the frameworks for telecommunications (launched by the landmark 1987 Green Paper on telecommunication, above) and for media (established by various Community legislative initiatives described in the earlier chapters). No doubt this area will develop considerably in the near future.

The media and data protection

The issue of data protection is an enormous one with implications far beyond the media. Nevertheless, it will be useful to include at this point a brief discussion of some of the implications of Community policies on data protection for the media, especially as this is an area where the more traditional media and new technology interact.

The Directive on the protection of individuals with regard to the processing of personal data and on the free movement of such data[45] has to be implemented in Member States by October 1998; a UK Bill to do so was published in January 1998. The Directive has, of course, a very wide scope, involving matters which are mainly outside the realm of audio-visual policy, and is indeed to a large degree based on earlier work of the Council of Europe. However, there is one respect in which it is highly relevant. Audio-visual media are used to disseminate information about individuals, both within Member States and within the Union (and indeed outside it). It was recognized that restrictions on the use of subject data might conflict with the principle of freedom of expression and rights of the media to gather information and to report on it. Therefore, in both the Recitals and within the Directive itself, there is special reference to the media and some degree of special provision for it.

45. Directive 95/46/EC of the European Parliament and of the Council of 24 October 1995 on the protection of individuals with regard to the processing of personal data and on the free movement of such data <http://www2.echo.lu/legal/en/dataprot/directiv/directiv.html>

Recital 17 stipulates that the principles of the Directive are to apply 'in a restricted manner', as laid down in art. 9, insofar as 'the processing of sound and image data carried out for purposes of journalism or the purposes of literary or artistic expression is concerned, in particular in the audiovisual field . . .' Article 9 itself provides that:

> Member States shall provide for exemptions or derogations from the provisions of this Chapter, Chapter IV and Chapter VI for the processing of personal data carried out solely for journalistic purposes or the purpose of artistic or literary expression only if they are necessary to reconcile the right to privacy with the rules governing freedom of expression.

There is a variety of different models within Member States as to how their data protection (and general) laws interact with and affect the right to freedom of expression, particularly on the part of media. The Working Party on the Protection of Individuals with regard to the Processing of Personal Data assessed the implications of art. 9, considering national models and the Council of Europe's Report on Data Protection and the Media of 1991, and a Recommendation was adopted by the Working Party on 25 February 1997 focussing on exemptions and derogations in relation to processing personal data for journalistic purposes.[46]

The Working Party notes that the European Convention on Human Rights establishes that, by art. 10, everyone has the right to freedom of expression, and that 'This right is one of the fundamental human rights deriving from the constitutional traditions common to the Member States and is one of the most characteristic elements of the legal heritage of democratic societies.' Article 8 of the same Convention guarantees the right to respect for private and family life, and for home and correspondence (see Chapter Three above). Data protection comes within the scope of the protection guaranteed under this article. Any limitations or derogations to either right must be prescribed by law and must respect the principle of proportionality. These norms are made part of Community law by art. F, para 2 of the Treaty on European Union which prescribes that the Union shall respect fundamental

---

[46.] Working Party on the Protection of Individuals with regard to the Processing of Personal Data Recommendation 1/97, *Data Protection Law and the Media*, adopted by the Working Party on 25 February 1997. http://www.open.gov.uk./dpr/d5012en.htm; all quotes are from this source.

rights as guaranteed by the European Convention on Human Rights and the constitutional traditions common to the Member States.

It might seem that the two rights to freedom of expression and to privacy conflict, but, in the view of the Working Party, '. . . the two fundamental rights must not be seen as inherently conflicting. In the absence of adequate safeguards for privacy individuals may be reluctant to freely express their ideas. Similarly identification and profiling of readers and users of information services is likely to reduce the willingness of individuals to receive and impart information.'

The principles that should be borne in mind, suggest the Working Party, in evaluating to what extent the application of the relevant provisions of the Directive needs to be limited in order to protect freedom of expression include the following:

- data protection law applies to the media in principle;
- derogations and exemptions may be granted only in relation to Chapter II on the general measures on legitimacy of data processing, Chapter IV on data transfers to third countries and Chapter VI on the powers of supervisory authorities;
- no derogation or exemption from the provisions on security of data may be granted;
- derogations and exemptions under art. 9 must follow the principle of proportionality, taking into account 'ethical and professional obligations of journalists as well as to the self-regulatory forms of supervision provided by the profession';
- derogations and exemptions cannot be granted to the media or to journalists as such, but only to anybody processing data for journalistic purposes including electronic publishing. Any other form of data processing by journalists or the media is subject to the ordinary rules of the directive. Thus, in relation to electronic publishing, processing of subscribers' data for billing, or processing for direct marketing purposes (including processing of data on media use for profiling purposes) fall under the ordinary data protection regime; and
- the Directive requires a balance to be struck between two fundamental freedoms. Limits to the right of access and rectification prior to publication 'could be proportionate only in so far as individuals enjoy the right to reply or obtain rectification of false information after publication'.

Conclusion

As with audiovisual matters we find a large number of Community activities being undertaken in relation to the information society. Indeed, the Commission deserves considerable credit for realizing the potential of media convergence early on and undertaking important studies about its implications, including social implications which have been neglected in many other discussions of the effects of the new media technology. Moreover, the success of telecommunications liberalization suggests that there is considerable potential for Community action here; at the very least competition law will have a major role to play in the new media world. The work on data protection also shows how issues of human rights may arise in this new context, perhaps unexpectedly.

During the early part of 1998, for example, the Community produced a number of opinions and position papers, principally with regard to the Internet and its general governance. The breadth of its concern was expressed thus:

> The European Community and the Member States have an abiding interest in the future organisation and management of the Internet because the structures that are put in place will strongly influence the highest level of decision, the extent to which all areas of the world – including Europe – have fair and equitable access to the Internet, the introduction of competition in those areas – such as the allocation of Domain Names – where this would be beneficial, and ultimately determine the general efficiency and economy of the Internet through responsibility for and control of essential co-ordination between the respective Internet bodies.[47]

Amongst the Community's main initiatives is the Communication from the Commission to the European Parliament, the Council, the Economic and Social Committee and the Committee of the regions on Globalisation and the Information Society: the Need for strengthened international coordination.[48]

Essentially, the Communication attempts to identify key issues that require 'strengthened international coordination' as regards the 'on-line economy', thus flagging-up the Commission's concern

---

[47.] Communication to the Council from the Commission. International policy issues related to Internet Governance. 20 February 1998 <http://www.ispo.cec.be/eif/policy/>

[48.] COM (98) 50 <http://www.ispo.cec.be/eif/policy/com9850en.html>

that a fundamental part of the information society is this specific economy – what it calls the 'global electronic marketplace'. Examples of legal issues to be addressed are: VAT (indirect taxation); jurisdiction; labour laws concerning teleworkers; copyright; trademarks; data protection; authentication; consumer protection; contractual terms and conditions; harmful and illegal content; and criminal law matters. The Community's 'big idea' is its proposal for an 'International Charter', to be adopted by or during 1999, which will elaborate how these, and other issues, will be coordinated at the international level. Such an approach is commended in preference to creating either a new international supervisory body or a set of new, binding rules.

Nevertheless, as the Green Paper suggests, there is still considerable uncertainty as to the approach to be taken for the future. This reflects a broader uncertainty about the extent of the media revolution caused by convergence, and as to the extent to which regulation will be necessary, and, if so, why. This leads us to our final chapter which will attempt to hazard some answers to these questions.

CHAPTER EIGHT

Conclusions

The end of 1997 sees media policy at a crossroads, and it is by no means easy to predict the future. Indeed, the Commission's Green Paper of that date makes this point by its very, and inevitable, vagueness. It seems clear that convergence is leading to the possibility of media which will be fundamentally different from those of the past when the policies and law described in this book were formed, and so it might be implied that media policy, despite, for example, the revision of the *Television Without Frontiers* Directive during 1997, is already outdated.

Indeed, there is an influential school of thought which predicts the imminent end of the traditional media scene.[1] It is predicted that, as a result of convergence and digitalization, new forms of media will replace the old and will permit far greater consumer control, both of channels received (through the proliferation of digital services) and of content (through further development of interactivity and the Internet). As a result, culture in its established sense (whether European or otherwise) will be replaced by a new diversity permitting consumer sovereignty. In a world where a viewer can receive 500 or more television channels, for example, there will be no need to protect key sporting events because everyone who wishes to view them will be able to subscribe to the relevant channels; indeed, because of the proliferation of specialized services far more material will be available to fit their interests. Moreover, ability to select material through interactivity and the Internet would simply remove the need for controls on content; broadcasting would become more like the content of a telephone message, traditionally outside the scope of governmental

---

[1.] For discussion, and criticism, of this school of thought see Goldberg, D., Prosser, T. and Verhulst, S., *Regulating the Changing Media: A Comparative Study*, Clarendon Press, 1998, esp. Chs. 1 and 9.

or supra-governmental scrutiny as a matter of private choice.

As a result of these developments, according to this view of the future of the media many of the concerns of the policies described in this book would seem like the last gasp of a dying era. For example, the protection of public service broadcasting opaquely given by the Treaty of Amsterdam would appear a doomed attempt to protect what will disappear by a process of natural evolution anyway. Permitting the protection of key sporting events for unencrypted viewing would seem to misunderstand fundamentally the market for sports rights and the ability of the new media to meet specialized needs, and the necessity of appropriate payment for doing so. The use of quotas of European material would on this view also fundamentally misunderstand an industry which is essentially multi-national in nature, and attempts to protect linguistic diversity are doomed in a media world which treats English as a universal language. Finally, it would seem hardly surprising that the Community has had difficulty in framing rules limiting the concentration of media ownership when, it is claimed, the key to success will be size and only large multinational enterprises will be able to compete effectively on world markets.

At first sight the implication of this view of the new media or 'information society' would seem to suggest that regulation is unnecessary and that the Community, like national governments, should simply sit back and let market forces have free rein. A moment's thought will however suggest that this is unworkable. Setting aside for the moment cultural concerns, a large proportion of the policies discussed in this book have been concerned not with limiting the operation of markets but with creating the preconditions for their successful operation and in particular for the continuance of their successful operation. This is most evident in the basic concern with freedom of movement of services, the major basis for *Television Without Frontiers*. It could be argued that this has now been achieved and that freedom to transmit and to receive broadcasts is now a reality throughout the European Union. However, the caselaw on the Directive suggests that the problems of freedom of transmission have not yet been fully solved, and it must not be forgotten that the Union will soon enlarge to include a number of nations in which competition in broadcasting is a relatively new experience, and where state-controlled broadcasters have long been used to a dominant role. At the very least, this could mean that assumptions of national preference continue to form an important part of national media policy, precisely what much of the policy discussed in this book has been directed against. As in so many other issues, enlargement of the Union will raise crucial new questions relevant to all the themes of this book.

The continuing relevance of Community law and policy in a new world of media consumer sovereignty is most apparent in the case of competition law. We have seen that so far it has had a relatively limited role in relation to the traditional media, partly because of the important role of public service there, partly because of difficulties in framing new roles on media ownership and partly because of difficulties in applying existing law, especially to mergers (though this has been partially remedied by recent changes to the thresholds determining Community jurisdiction over mergers). However, as suggested above, the 'new media' are becoming closer to telecommunications than to broadcasting in its traditional sense. We have seen that competition law and policy within the Community have had a fundamental role to play in creating open markets for telecommunications services; indeed, this could be claimed to be the most successful of any of the policy areas described in this book. It is quite clear that Community law will continue to be of importance in policing the liberalized telecommunications markets, for example in ensuring fair arrangements for interconnection between competing operators, and indeed one of the successes of the liberalization process has been to force more thinking to take place on the best regulatory regimes to be adopted after liberalization. This also finds its expression in the convergence Green Paper where the establishment of effective and independent regulators is seen as required by the increased competition brought on by convergence. Moreover, Community action has already been taken on some of the key areas of convergence between broadcasting and telecommunications, most notably in the case of attempting to ensure non-discriminatory access to digital services. On a somewhat different issue, the successful operation of new media markets will be dependent on the development of effective and clear rules on intellectual property on which, after a slow start, the Community has been able to make some contribution.

Finally, it is noticeable that the Commission has been relatively early to appreciate the social implications of the information society, and has devoted considerable effort to the study of the employment, political and cultural effects of convergence, while its efforts to ensure data protection have been more advanced than those of many Member States, let alone those of potential entrants to the Union.

Overall, then, even if we are witnessing a revolutionary change from traditional media to the information society, this will not render all aspects of Community media policy redundant. A substantial proportion of the initiatives already taken will retain their importance, notably competition law will retain its role even in a world of consumer sovereignty, whilst the Commission has been at the forefront of attempts to assess the implications of such a revolutionary change.

We can go further, however, in suggesting that Community media policy will retain its importance in the future media world. To suggest that the process is one of revolution, determined by technological advance, which simply **replaces** traditional media by new forms subject to consumer sovereignty, is to offer a very one-sided picture of current developments. To suggest that the technological opportunities opened up by convergence will automatically be taken up is to misunderstand the overall nature of the media which is likely to remain mixed for a considerable period in the future. Thus convergence of media themselves (rather than merely of the technologies which make them possible) is a gradual process and one which has occurred to a different degree in different nations. In the majority of cases, the traditional media, including public service broadcasting, are likely to retain a major role for the foreseeable future. Indeed, some of the least successful aspects of Community policy such as the attempt to promote High Definition Television failed in part because of an over-willingness to promote a particular technological solution without considering consumer demand for it. This suggests some of the principles associated with Community policy will not necessarily lose their relevance with the development of media convergence; for example, cultural concerns and concern about the effects of violent or sexually explicit content, or of hate speech, will not disappear in the atomized marketplace.

It is of course easy to dismiss some of the earlier attempts at integration through a Community culture, for example the European television channel, as naïve and outdated. Nevertheless, it is possible to argue that concepts such as public service or broadcasting as a means of reference to a common national or supra-national culture have a certain value **alongside** the atomized world of consumer sovereignty. For example, the consumer choice offered among competing channels assumes that we all know what we want in advance through having predefined preferences for which we are prepared to buy services. An advantage of the traditional model of public service broadcasting in which a mix of different types of programme was required was precisely that we learn through coming across the unexpected. Thus recent developments such as the Public Broadcasting Protocol to the Treaty of Amsterdam and the protection of important sporting events can be seen not as the last gasp of a dying culture but as an attempt to defend the continuing existence of a different broadcasting culture, whose existence alongside the new forms of media which is essential to preserve real diversity. Even the controversial quotas on European materials, and the less controversial programmes of financial and other support to European media content industries, can be defended on the grounds that it is difficult to offer a real choice of cultural material if all that is available is American, even if economic factors such as economies of scale in the national market would give United States productions considerable economic advantages.

The argument then, is that the future of Community media policy is unlikely to be merely one of creating and policing the competitive marketplace of media plenty; although cultural concerns may have been handled in a naïve fashion in the past, they have not become irrelevant. More precise concerns can also be identified which do not simply involve policing the marketplace. As we have seen, one of the peculiarities of the media as a subject of policy is that human rights have an especially high salience here, notably the right to freedom of expression but also that of privacy. Thus the European Convention on Human Rights has often proved an important source of principle in areas as diverse as freedom of transmission and reception, controls on content and data protection. In domestic media law, constitutional courts have often played a major role in defining and enforcing these rights, for example in Germany, Italy or the United States.[2] In recent years there has been an increasing consciousness of the importance of the role of rights, especially Convention rights, in the European Community and Community law may have advantages as a means of enforcing these rights in particular circumstances through ensuring the availability of remedies in national courts and through pro-

---

[2.] See *ibid.*, chs. 2, 3 and 7; Craufurd Smith, *op. cit.*

viding a more effective supra-national constraint on unwilling national governments. Thus we can expect the role of Community law as an implementor of basic rights, especially those derived from the Convention, to continue in future. Indeed, the familiar process of the balancing of rights in ways not analogous to the operation of the marketplace will become more rather than less pressing as media convergence develops further. For example, digital satellite television is likely to lead to more problems of attempts by Member States to prevent pornographic programming being transmitted from other States, a classic example of the conflict between freedom of expression and its limitations. Pornography on the Internet, including child pornography, is becoming a larger, not a smaller concern and again involves classic issues of the conflicts between, and limitations on, rights. As was documented at the end of the previous chapter, data protection may involve for the media a very strong tension between freedom of expression and of privacy rights, and it has been up to the Community to provide guidance on how that should be resolved, basing its own action on earlier work of the Council of Europe. Thus the human rights dimension of media law and regulation, including that of the Community, seems set to develop in the future.

Perhaps ironically, some of the older desire to protect public service broadcasting has emerged in a different form in telecommunications liberalization and in the Green Paper on convergence. Thus one of the key themes in the liberalization process has been that of ensuring that universal service is protected, or indeed in some Member States that universal service is enhanced. This was defined as 'making available a defined minimum service of specified quality to all users at an affordable price', though later definitions have become more demanding.[3] This is then essentially a social concern based on a desire for social integration of the population through inclusiveness in service provision. Such concerns also underlay the revision of the *Television Without Frontiers* Directive in such a way as to permit attempts to preserve universal access to important sporting events in unencrypted form. Similar principles are evident in the Green Paper and are seen by the Commission as essential elements in enabling everyone to participate in

---

3. *Developing Universal Service for Telecommunications in a Competitive Environment*, COM(93)159 (final). See also the *Communication on Universal Service in Telecommunications* COM(96)73.

the information society; indeed, convergence is seen as enabling new forms of participation to be offered. Again, there appears to be a central element of Community policy here which is not simply concerned to ensure that markets work freely but to supplement them with principles of social solidarity. Indeed, the minor amendments made by the Amsterdam Treaty with the purpose of protecting public service reflect a feeling, especially by some Continental Member States, that universal service does not go far enough in protecting social solidarity and equal access to public services.

The outcome of these reflections is that the themes encountered in Community media policy as described in this book are perennial ones and are not likely to disappear with further media convergence. Clearly the process has involved some serious errors, such as the early stress on the importance of a Community television channel as a means of cultural integration and the later support for questionable new technologies, in particular High Definition Television in the form envisaged by the Commission. Nevertheless, the Community should be given credit for having successfully grasped issues central to any media regulation and for, on the whole, having dealt with them successfully. This has occurred despite the problems of mixed rationales for action, difficulties in defining the appropriate Community competence, failures of some individual ventures and opposition and scepticism from some Member States. Important issues have not been fully resolved, notably copyright, and as yet the approach to be taken to the information society remains vague. However, the record of many Member States has been worse. The next few years after 1997 will be crucial and fascinating in determining the continuing future role of Community media law and regulation, but we hope we have suggested in this work that it has considerable potential.

Further reading

For a regular update on European media law and policy issues see IRIS: *Legal Observations of the European Audiovisual Observatory. 77 Rue de la Robertsau F-67000 Strasbourg, Tel +33 388 144408, Fax +33 388 144419*

Collins, R., *Broadcasting and Audiovisual Policy in the European Single Market* (John Libbey, 1994).

Craufurd Smith, R., *Broadcasting Law and Fundamental Rights* (Clarendon Press, 1997).

Hoffman-Riem, W., *Regulating Media: The Licensing and Supervision of Broadcasting in Six Countries*, Guilford Communication Series, (Guilford Press, 1996).

Hondius, F., 'Regulating Transfrontier Television – the Strasbourg Option', *Yearbook of European Law*, **8** (1988).

Humphreys, P.J., *Mass Media and Media Policy in Western Europe* (Manchester University Press, 1996).

White, S., Bate, S., and Johnson, T., *Satellite Communications in Europe: Law and Regulation*, FT Law & Tax **145**, (1996).

Winn, D., *European Community and International Media Law*, European Business Law & Practice Series (Kluwer Law Intl., 1993).

Bibliography

Bangemann, M., *et al.*, 'Europe and the global information society: Recommendations to the European Council', a report prepared for the European Council meeting (1994) 24–5

Barendt, E., *Broadcasting Law: A Comparative Study*, Oxford University Press, 1995

Barendt, E. (ed.), *Year Book of Media and Entertainment Law*; v. 1 & 2, Oxford University Press, 1996, 1997

Beltrane, F., 'Harmonising Media Ownership Rules: Problems and Prospects', *Utilities Law Review* **7** (1996) 172

Building the European information superhighway for us all: First reflections of the High Level Group of Experts, Interim report, Brussels, January 1996

Burgelman, J.C. and Pauwels, C., 'La convergence de l'audiovisuel et des télécommunications en Europe' in *La politique des Communautés Européennes*, Lentic, 1990

Campbell, C., (ed.) *International Media Liability: Civil Liability in the Information Age,* Wiley & Sons, 1997

Coleman J. and Rollet B., *Television in Europe*, Intellect, 1997

Collins, R., *Broadcasting and Audiovisual Policy in the European Single Market*, John Libbey, 1994

Craufurd Smith, R., *Broadcasting Law and Fundamental Rights*, Clarendon Press, 1997

Dai, X., Cawson, A. and Holmes, P., 'The Rise and Fall of High Definition Television: The Impact of European Technology Policy', *Journal of Common Market Studies* **34(2)** (1996) 149

de Moragas Spa, M. and Garitaonandia, C., *Decentralization in the Global Era, Television in the Regions, Nationalities and Small Countries of the European Union*, John Libbey, 1995

Doyle, G., 'From "Pluralism" to "Ownership": Europe's emergent policy on media concentrations navigates the doldrums' *The Journal of Information, Law and Technology*, (3) (1997)

Euromedia Research Group, *The Media in Western Europe. The Euromedia Handbook*, Sage, 1997

The European Convention on Transfrontier Television, *European Treaty Series* (1989) no. 132

Eurostat, *Audio-visual Statistics – Report 1995*, Eurostat, 1995

Goldberg, D., Prosser, T. and Verhulst, S., *Regulating the Changing Media: A Comparative Study*, Oxford University Press, 1998

Harcourt A.J., 'Regulating for Media Concentration: the Emerging Policy of the European Union', *Utilities Law Review* 7 (1996) 202

Hirsch, M. and Petersen, V.G., 'Regulation of Media at the European Level', *Dynamics of Media Politics. Broadcast and Electronic Media in Western Europe*, Sage, 1992

Hitchens, L., 'Media Ownership and Control: A European Approach', *The Modern Law Review* 57 (1994) 585

Hitchens, L., 'Identifying European Community Audio-visual Policy in the Dawn of the Information Society', *Yearbook of Media and Entertainment Law* 2 (1996) 45

Hoffman-Riem, W., *Regulating Media: The Licensing and Supervision of Broadcasting in Six Countries*, Guilford Communication Series, Guilford Press, 1996

Hondius, F., 'Regulating Transfrontier Television – the Strasbourg Option', *Yearbook of European Law* 8 (1988)

Humphreys, P.J., *Mass Media and Media Policy in Western Europe*, Manchester University Press, 1996

Hunt, A., 'Regulation of Telecommunications: the Developing EU Regulatory Framework and its Impact on the United Kingdom', *European Public Law* 3 (1997) 93

Information Society Forum, 'Networks for People and their Communities. Making the Most of the Information Society in the European Union', First Annual Report to the European Commission from the Information Society Forum, June 1996

Kamall, S., *Spicer's European Union Policy Briefings, Telecommunications Policy*, Cartermill Publishing, 1996

KPMG, *Public Policy Issues Arising from Telecommunications and Audio-visual Convergence*, Report for the European Commission, KPMG, 1996

KPMG, *The Single Market Review Series, Subseries II – Impact on Services, Audio-visual Services and Production*, KPMG, 1996

Maggiore, M., 'The technological challenge', chapter 4 in *Broadcasting and Audiovisual Policy in the European Single Market*, John Libbey, 1994

Maggiore, M., *Audiovisual Production in the Single Market*, CEC, 1990

McGonagle, M., (ed.), *A Textbook on Media Law,* Gill & MacMillan Ltd, 1996

Negrine, R. and Papthanassopoulos, S., *The Internationalisation of Television*, Pinter, 1990

Paraschos, E., *Media Law and Regulation in the European Union: National, Transnational and US Perspectives*, Iowa State University Press, 1997

Porter, V., 'Film and Television in the Single European Market: Dreams and Delusions', Inaugural Professorial Lecture, 17 October 1991

Prosser, T., Goldberg, D. and Verhulst, S., *The Impact of New Communications Technologies and Media Concentrations and Pluralism*, Strasbourg: Council of Europe (1997) MM-CM (96) 3

Sanchez-Taberno, A., *Media Concentration in Europe: Commercial Enterprise and the Public Interest*, Media Monograph No 16, The European Institute for the Media, 1993

Schlesinger, P., 'From cultural defence to political cultures: media, politics and collective identity in the European Union' *Media, Culture and Society* **19** (1997) 369

Schoof, H. and Watson Brown, A., 'Information highways and media policies in the European Union', *Telecommunications Policy* **19**(4) (1995) 325

Schulze, M., 'Developments in the field of European copyright law: The Magill and SACEM Judgements, Contents and Application of the Various Directives in the Field of Copyright Law' in *Legal Developments in the Audio-visual Sector*, IRIS, 1995

Schwartz, I., 'Broadcasting Without Frontiers in the European Community' *Journal of Media Law and Practice* **6**(1) (1985) 26

Scott, C., *Competition and Coordination: Their Role in the Future of European Community Telecommunications Regulation*, Centre for the Study of Regulated Industries, 1995

Servan-Schreiber, J., *Le Défi Américain – The American Challenge*, Penguin, 1968

Siune, K. and Truetzschler, W., *Dynamics of Media Politics: Broadcast and Electronic Media in Western Europe*, Sage, 1992

Status Report On European Union Telecommunications Policy, Brussels, May 1997

Ungerer, H., 'EU Competition Law in the Telecommunications, Media and Information Technology Sectors', Fordham Corporate Law Institute 22nd Annual Conference on International Antitrust Law & Policy, Fordham University School of Law, 27 October 1995

van Eijk, N., 'Liberalisation of Cable Television Networks in Europe' in *Legal Developments in the Audio-visual Sector*, IRIS, 1995

Verhulst, S., 'Public Service Broadcasting in Europe', *Utilities Law Review* **8**(2) (1997) 31

Verhulst, S. and Goldberg, D., 'European Media Policy: Complexity and Comprehensiveness, ch. 1 in d'Haenens, L. and Saeys, F., *Media Dyna-*

mics and Regulatory Concerns in the Digital Age, Berlin, 1998

Voorhoof, D., 'Critical perspectives on the scope and the application of Article 10 of the European Convention on Human Rights', *Mass Media Files No 10,* Council of Europe Press, 1995

Wallace, R. and Goldberg, D., 'Television Broadcasting: the Community's Response', *Common Market Law Review* **26** (1989) 717

Wallace, R. and Goldberg, D., *Regulating the Audiovisual Industry: the Second Phase*, Butterworths, 1991

Wallace, R. and Goldberg, D., 'The EEC Directive on Television Broadcasting', *Yearbook of European Law* **9** (1989) 175

Watson, A., 'Mutual recognition of licences for satellite broadcasting and regulatory framework for digital television' in *Legal Developments in the Audio-visual Sector*, IRIS, 1995

Weatherill, S., *Law and the Integration in the European Union*, Clarendon, 1995

Weymouth, T. and Lamizet, B., (eds), *Markets and Myths: Forces for Change in the European Media*, Addison Wesley Longman, 1997

White, S., Bate, S. and Johnson, T., *Satellite Communications in Europe: Law and Regulation*, FT Law & Tax, 1996, p. 145

Wilkins, K.L., 'Television Without Frontiers: An EEC Broadcasting Premiere', *Boston College International and Comparative Law Review* **16** (1991) 195

Index

abuse of a dominant position, 88, 89
accounting separation, 78
ACTS Programme, 109
Advanced Television Standards
    Directive, 85, 92–3
advertising, 31–2, 49, 64–5, 69–70,
    73–4, 74–5, 93–5
Amsterdam Treaty, 4, 11, 19–20, 92,
    123, 126, 128
antennae, 76
anti-competitive agreements, 89
Audio-visual EUREKA, 53, 82–3

Bangemann, M., 97, 101
Bangemann report, 97–9
Bertelsmann Group, 89
broadcasting, definition of, 60
*Building the European Information
    Society for us all*, 111

cable television, 46, 71, 72–3, 76–8, 87
cinema, 30–1, 63–4, 81, 83, 113
commercial communications *see*
    advertising
Committee of the Regions, 23–4
competition law, 2, 88–93, 124
concentration *see* ownership
conditional access, 85–6, 92–3
constitutional courts, 4, 126
Contact Committee, 67–8
convergence, 96–7, 125 *see also* Green
    Paper on Convergence
copyright, 49–51, 86–8, 124
    Directives, 87–8
Council of Europe
    Action Plan on the information
        society, 36–8
    agreements of, 27–8

Convention on Transfrontier
    Television, 5, 29–33, 60
data protection, 117–18
information society, 36–8
Intergovernmental Cooperation
    programme, 25
objectives of, 26,
organisation of, 25–7, 32–3,
recommendations of, 28–9
Standing Committee (T-TT), 32
Steering Committee on the Mass
    Media (CDMM), 26–7
see also European Convention on
    Human Rights, freedom of
    expression, privacy
Council of Ministers, 44
culture article 17–19

data protection, 117–19
databases, 87
de Deus Pinheiro, Joao, 65–6
decoders, 85–6, 92–3
Delors, Jacques, 11
Deutsche Bundespost Telekom, 89
digital television, 1, 2, 85–6, 89, 127
    see also conditional access,
    decoders
Digital Video Broadcasting Group
    (DVB), 85
discrimination, prohibition of, 46–8

Economic and Social Committee
    (ECOSOC), 23, 82
encryption, 85–6
enlargement of the European Union,
    123–4
ESPRIT, 109
European Audiovisual Dimension, 83

European Audiovisual Observatory, 38, 83
European broadcasting channel, 3, 44, 125
European Broadcasting Union (EBU), 10, 39
European Commission, 21
  competition policy, 89–90
European Community
  audio-visual policy, 8–11
  competence of, 6, 11–20
European Convention on Human Rights, 4–5, 25, 33–6, 45, 118–19, 126–7
European Court of Human Rights, 34–6
European Court of Justice, 1, 9, 22–3, 57, 60–1, 88
  and *Television Without Frontiers* Directive, 68–75
European Group of Television Advertising, 39
European Group on Ethics in Science and New Technologies, 112–14
European Guarantee Fund, 80, 81–2
European Parliament, 10, 14, 21–2, 42–5,
  quotas, 63
  resolutions on radio and television broadcasting, 42–3, 44
European Platform of Regulatory Authorities (EPRA), 40
European Radiocommunications Office (ERO), 40–1
European Telecommunications Standards Institute, 105–6
Europes Way to the Information Society. Action Plan, 98–9

freedom of expression, 33–6, 58
freedom of transmission, 45–7 *see also* *Television Without Frontiers* Directive
freedom to provide services, 2, 9, 13, 14, 16, 45–8, 78, 123

gateway monopolies, 37 *see also* conditional access, decoders
General Agreement on Tariffs and Trade (GATT) 62–3
Green Paper on convergence of telecommunications, media and information technology, 114–17, 122, 124, 127–8

Green Paper on pluralism and media concentration, 90–1
Green Paper on telecommunications services, 105–6
Green Paper on the establishment of a common market for broadcasting, 12, 13, 15, 45–51

Hahn Report and resolution of the European Parliament, 42–3
High Definition Television (HDTV), 2, 54, 83–5, 125, 128
High Level Expert Group on the social and societal aspects of the information society, 111–12
High Level Think Tank on Future Audiovisual Policy of the European Union, 113
Holland Media Group, 89–90
House of Lords Select Committee on the European Communities, 12–15, 50–1

INFO2000, 110
information society, 2, 7, 88, 96–121
  conferences on, 102
  employment implications, 111–12
  regulation of, 103–4, 114–17
  social aspects of, 111–14, 124–5
  support for industry, 109–10
Information Society Forum, 99, 112
Information Society Project Office, 98
institutional conflict, 5, 20–4
intellectual property *see* copyright
interconnection, 106–7, 108–9
Internet, 3, 79, 120–1 *see also* information society

journalism, 117–19

linguistic policy, 62, 63–4
Learning in the information society initiative, 100–1

MAC standard, 84–5
media
  coverage of, 8–9
  cultural dimension of, 2–3, 17–19, 43, 91–2, 125
  moral dimension of, 3, 30, 65–7, 125
MEDIA programme, 51–3, 79–82
MEDIAII, 80–2
mergers, 89–90 *see also* ownership

minors, protection of, 65–7, 74–5, 79
misleading advertising, 93–4
Mitterrand, F., 43
Multilingual Information Society
     (MLIS) Programme, 110
Open Network Provision, 105, 106,
     107–9
Oreja, Marcelio, 21
Organization for Security and
     Cooperation in Europe (OSCE),
     38–9
ownership, 88–91, 123

pay-tv, 85–6 *see also* conditional
     access
pluralism *see* ownership
pornography, 3, 30, 65–7, 127
privacy, 34, 101, 117–19
prizes and festivals, 83
programme content, 30, 48, 65–6, 79,
     122–3 *see also* minors, privacy,
     pornography, right of reply
proportionality, 118–19
public service, 2, 11, 20,
public service broadcasting, 4, 5,
     19–20, 92, 123, 126

quotas 30, 61–63, 123, 126

RACE Programme, 109
regional policies, 23–4, 112
Rendez–Vous Television, 66–7
right of reply, 48, 67

satellite television, 3, 76 8, 87, 127
Schwartz, I., 15–16, 45, 47
self-regulation, 79, 93–4, 121
single market, 45
spectrum management, 40–1
sponsorship, 32, 39, 64–5, 73–4 *see
     also* advertising
sporting events, access to 30, 59, 61,
     123
state aids, 91–2
support systems for industry
     development of, 79–83

information society, 109–10
     origins of, 51–3
technical programmes
     origins of, 53–4
     standardisation, 83–6
telecommunications liberalisation, 1,
     77–8, 100, 104–9, 124 *see also*
     interconnection, universal service
Telematics programme, 110
teleshopping, 59, 64–5, 73, 77
Television Without Frontiers Directive,
     1, 22, 56–68, 95, 122
     advertising, 64–5, 69–70, 73–4,
          74–5
     application of, 67–8
     caselaw on, 68–75
     coverage of, 59–68
     definition of broadcasting, 60
     independent productions, 61, 63
     jurisdiction over broadcasters,
          60–1, 70–1, 72–3
     minors, protection of, 65–7, 74–5
     national authorities powers, 61,
          69–70, 70–1, 72–3, 74–5
     principles of, 57–8
     quotas for European and
          independent works, 61–3
     rebroadcasting of films, 63–4
     revision of, 58–9, 127
     right of reply, 67
     teleshopping, 59, 64–5, 73, 77
TEN-TELECOM Programme, 110
tobacco advertising, 31, 94
Tongue Report 20

United States, 10, 62, 126
universal service, 108–9, 127

V-chip, 59, 65

Working Party on the Protection of
     Individuals with regard to the
     Processing of Personal Data, 118–19
World Trade Organisation, 21, 109

XXXTV, 66–7